Dr. Lydia A. Duggins has broken new ground.

Since 1954 in tests covering every walk of life from the mentally retarded to the very gifted, her perceptually-oriented approach has proven its merit.

Dr. Duggins has tossed away the traditional concepts of learning by rote or by a series of imposed rules, and substituted instead the child's own developmental growth patterns. Her method utilizes the child's speech and relates his unique experiences to the development of "talk on paper", or reading.

Now for the first time the entire reading experience is internalized into the very being of the child. He is encouraged to utilize his hands and feet in developing the spatial relationships of reading and to act out each concept through the muscles of his body. A word becomes something a child can feel and manipulate as well as something he sees.

No longer need a child be exposed to language already structured according to rules he must memorize and comprehend later. The reading experience is exploratory. The child takes the raw materials of language and forms patterns based on his own ideas and background. Thus, the differences in readiness for learning and the rate of learning is "built in" to the approach and not imposed upon it by artificial means.

Developing Children's Perceptual Skills in Reading steps heavily upon many established beliefs, but the enthusiastic reception given the Duggins method is ample testimony that the educational community is ready and willing to accept a successful innovation.

DEVELOPING CHILDREN'S PERCEPTUAL SKILLS IN READING

Dr. Lydia A. Duggins

DEVELOPING CHILDREN'S PERCEPTUAL SKILLS IN READING

Illustrated by Susan Purdy

MEDIAX Inc. *Publisher*

Box 549, Wilton, Conn. 06897

Printed in the U.S.A.

Library of Congress Catalog Card Number: 70-81156

Some Preliminary Thoughts

1. *Developing Children's Perceptual Skills in Reading*

The method presented in the following pages is derived from years of research and study. It is a method that makes reading part of the child's whole makeup because it employs the child's own developmental growth patterns. The method is based upon the child's speech, and relates his own experiences in the sorting and manipulating functions of speech to the development of the patterns of "talk on paper" or reading.

We have found that motor-perceptual growth in reading is the formation of response patterns into clusters of habit systems which go from general to specific and from specific to general; thus, the responses required in reading are highly selective in nature. A child must first learn the response patterns and then the selective use of these patterns.

Certain skills of visual space, knowing where, how many, and what symbols stand for the sounds in a word, and the rhythmic relationship of these sounds in a sequential pattern are fundamental to optimum growth in learning to read. Creative reading does not grow out of the *utilization* of vision, but rather the *function* of vision supported by a strong framework of sensory patterns that emerge from the child's total function. A child must internalize the patterns of reading, and these must be integrated into all the patterns he has developed in learning to talk.

When the foundations the child has built in speech are linked with the instruction he receives in reading, this instruction will be individualized and in harmony with the child's growth pattern, basic desires, and needs.

The basic building materials used for the reading program are the vowel sounds which are first experienced by the young child in the process of learning to talk. This speech process develops through control of the muscles of the child's body into patterns which become the basis for all communication through writing, listening, and reading. The development of reading skills involves the use of selected speech skills the child has achieved from his physical growth and environmental opportunity.

In the perceptually oriented teaching of reading, experiences for the child are thus internalized or incorporated into the physical patterns of his body. These experiences are exploratory. Rather than being told about it, the child finds out about it.

In this method, we have, therefore, two major premises:

a. *The reading experience for the child will be internalized.* To internalize the reading experience for the child means to incorporate it into the very muscles of his body; to utilize his hands and feet in developing the spatial relationships of reading. A word will become something a child can feel and manipulate as well as something he sees.

b. *The reading experience for the child will be exploratory.* The child will take the raw materials of language and form patterns for himself rather than be exposed to language already structured according to rules he must memorize and comprehend later.

A major goal of any reading program is the development of a sense of pattern or an awareness of organization in verbal materials. A pupil's communication abilities, not only in reading, but in writing, speaking, and listening, depend upon the achievement of this goal. The sense of pattern which is necessary for effective reading is built by strengthening the mental skills of associational relationships, paired comparisons, and categorizing.

By patterning our thinking into verbal concepts, these three mental patterns—associating relationships, categorizing and paired comparisons—enable us to extend our experiences through reading. We utilize these extended experiences to enrich our functions of living and, most hopefully, in communicating more understandingly with others and in comprehending their communication with us.

No thinking behavior can be classified into pure factors or units, but must necessarily contain some residue of all mental activity which has been experienced. The teacher, when asking for a pupil's response, merely gives a specific direction to the child's thinking about his individual store of mental information.

We know that we build the word symbols (or sight-insight skills of communication) on the sound and feeling of the child's spoken language. Therefore, we start here to pattern our lessons. What mode of communication will we use? *Talking*. Then we relate this to *writing*. *Writing* is *talking* on paper. To accomplish what objective? To the end that both we and others can *hear* what we have *said*. This leads us to *listening* to the sound of spoken language and eventually to *listening to books* or *reading*. In the act of reading we see and hear language simultaneously.

A further objective is to teach an understanding of written sentences by relating them to oral language or speech.

How are spoken sentences (talking) like written sentences (talking on paper)?

They both involve the use of words in a pattern of order and relationships.

They both involve the motor experience of feeling letter shapes.

They both utilize the child's storehouse of meanings and experiences.

Note that these three factors involve sound and feeling experiences primarily because these are the linking factors in speech and writing. They are the links in the chain of associations by which the child will begin with one series of experiences and use these to develop and strengthen another. They are his speech-bridge into reading.

In summary, the perceptually oriented approach may be contrasted to the traditional approaches as follows:

In the traditional approach	*In the perceptually oriented approach*
Left-right orientation is developed through a series of planned exercises, games, and the utilization of such devices as a pointer, arrows drawn on the child's paper.	Left-right orientation is developed through body imagery and related to space references such as beginning-middle-end. The child finds with his hands where a sound is located. He relates this to his ears rather than his eyes.

Learning the names of the letters is done by rote and by games that are largely visual in nature.	The child incorporates the letters into body experiences by acting out the form of the letters and by exploring this form through creative drawings.
Vowels and consonants are taught through a series of exercises in which the consonants and vowels are taught separately and the determination of the vowel sound is through a series of imposed rules, whereby the child is enabled to "sound out a word."	Vowels are taught through body imagery, involving the hands and ears and the whole body in relation to objects in the environment. Syllables are taught by utilizing the names of the consonants to show the relationship of consonant to vowel. This relationship is explored through writing and the sound of the vowel is determined by this relationship and employing no rules. The child is helped to hear the word rather than to sound it out.
Comprehension is taught largely through having the child read pre-patterned material and answer prepatterned questions.	Comprehension is developed by the verbal exploration of patterns of thinking about ideas, the manipulation of these ideas through linked thinking, categories, and paired comparisons; the raising of questions rather than the answering of them; and through further exploration of patterns and relationships through writing. Study skills are experienced rather than taught.

The perceptually oriented approach to the teaching of reading offers many advantages to the teacher:

1. Adjustment to individual differences in readiness for learning and rate of learning is "built in" to the approach rather than imposed upon it by artificial devices.
2. The major materials utilized by such an approach are a child, a teacher, and writing materials. It is therefore not

subject to the lag in keeping up with new ideas necessarily imposed upon published materials.

3. Vocabulary need not be controlled and much more variety can be offered to the child in content in his reading. The basal vocabulary becomes the child's speaking vocabulary and growth in reading is determined by the child's ability to grow.

2. *The Development and Analysis of the Methods Presented*

The methods presented in *Developing Children's Perceptual Skills in Reading* were formulated through informal exploratory studies from 1950 to 1954, and through experimental programs from 1955 to 1968. These studies were carried out in first grade classrooms in public schools in Memphis, Tennessee; Southeastern Louisiana; Connecticut, and New York.

The perceptual basis for the program in reading was described in *"Auditory Perception in the Beginning Reading Program"* (2),* and in *The Reading Teachers' Reader* (3).*

In the Louisiana studies 1955-1958 the results obtained from experimentation with children in first grade classrooms were related to the needs of children at the second, third, and fourth grade levels. Primary emphasis was upon the utilization of these skills in building good reading comprehension. The results of these studies were published in *"A Sequential Program for the Development of Skills in Spatial Relationships and Closure as a Basis for Reading Comprehension."*(1)*

A continuation of research studies in Connecticut in public school programs in Milford, Bridgeport, Trumbull, Fairfield, Stamford, Ridgefield, Westport, Bethel, Monroe, Waterbury, Greenwich, Easton and Norwalk and in Carmel, New York, led to further modifications of the structure of the program, especially in the relating of the reading instruction to children's developmental growth patterns in reading. These modifications were presented in *"Relating Reading Instruction to Children's Developmental Growth Patterns."*(4)* Finally, an analysis and evaluation of the experimental basis was presented in *Handbook of Research on Teaching.*(5)*

* Reference numbers (1), (2), (3), (4) and (5) refer to corresponding numbers in Bibliography on page 96.

Contents

CHAPTER 1

Preparation

Background

It is unnecessary to stress the importance of reading throughout our entire lives. As teachers, we are completely aware of the tremendous role it plays not only in successful achievement, but in personal satisfaction as well.

Teaching a child to read is probably the greatest single contribution we can make to a child's development, and every child, physically able, can learn to read.

It is the purpose of this book to teach children to read through the use of the same perceptual skills developed initially in learning to talk.

Determining the Child's Readiness in Speech

The first step is to listen to your children talk. Listen to them for a whole day. Really listen. Don't be obvious about it. You want to see how each child talks naturally. Listen for these things:

1. Does he talk in complete sentences?
   "Let's go" is a complete sentence; "go" is not.
   "I don't wanta" is a complete sentence;
   "don't wanta" is not.

2. Does he say all of a word?
   "floor," not "four."
   "going," not "goin."

If the answer to either of these questions is "no," don't tell him how to talk. Show him by repeating the word or sentence carefully. A child talks the way he hears other people talk. Be patient and friendly. A happy, confident child talks and reads better.

Some Rules to Consider

If the answer to these two questions is "yes," you are ready to start teaching him to read. Every child can read as well as he can talk. This is our goal:

Talk into reading
Reading into talk

But his talk is not yours. As long as you remember this, you will not harm a child by teaching him to read.

Before you start teaching your children the perceptual skills of reading, there are some rules you should observe. The success of your work will depend on the extent to which you remember and follow these.

1. Teach the children every day and, if possible, at the same time. Teach each skill to the entire class first. Later, small groups may have special help as needed.

2. Teach only one thing at a time.

3. Stop when your children get tired. Ten minutes a day is long enough for most children.

4. Tell a child he is doing fine. Do this no matter how many errors he makes. Never point out his mistakes.

5. Don't go to the next step until your children are proficient in the step on which you are working. Review steps frequently. Give special help to individual children or to small groups when needed.

The Library as an Aid

Take your children to the school library and let them select books to read. It doesn't matter that they can't read. You are building a habit. You are helping your children to find out what reading is about. You are helping them to read by sharing books with them.

Don't hover over your children while they select their books. You select a book for yourself; an adult book you intended to read for a long time but never got around to reading.

At the beginning of the daily reading period, get your book and have your children get theirs. You read your book and let them "read" theirs. Don't teach a child his book. Keep your hands off it. Read your own book.

This works like magic in setting up the reading habit and helping children to see themselves as readers. It won't work, however, if you don't enjoy your own book enough to tell them not to bother you while you are reading.

CHAPTER 2

Things to Do While Teaching Children the Perceptual Skills in Reading

How to Use the Activities

In this chapter, you will find out about the things to do with children while they are learning to read. These activities will help children tie together all the skills they will learn. Use them as often as you can, and as often as you feel necessary with your group. They may be carried out with the entire class or with small groups of children having special needs.

Reading as an Aid in Developing Perceptual Skills

Read to your children. As soon as you start teaching your children the names of the letters of the alphabet, Skill I, you should start reading to them as well as with them. Have the children select the book you will read to them.

Read books they can grow by. Because of the things they see on television, the things they hear on radio, and the more complex studies they have in school, children today have much more sophisticated tastes in books. If your children are to enjoy a book, it must have a plot that will compete with stories of men in space. A good rule to follow is this: Don't read a book to your children if you, yourself, are bored by it.

Even very young children enjoy such books as *Robinson Crusoe, Huckleberry Finn, Gulliver's Travels, The Wizard of Oz,* and *Alice in Wonderland*. Ask the librarian in the school library to help you select books you and your children will enjoy reading together.

Before you read a selection to your children, pick out a list of interesting words from it to share with them. Choose words of different lengths. For example, you might choose the following list from *Alice in Wonderland:*

astonishment	(4 syllables)
grin	(1 syllable)
wonderland	(3 syllables)
pensive	(2 syllables)

These are the syllables you say in a word. The number of syllables may not agree with the dictionary, but the syllables as shown in the dictionary are for writing words, not for reading them. We are using children's talk to reach them in order to hear books. If you are not sure of the number of syllables in a words as it is spoken, you can use this simple rule:

Count the vowels.
Two vowels together, such as the oa in the word boat, count as one, because they say only one.
The letter e at the end of a word doesn't count since you do not say it.

As you read to your children, give them the meaning of the word without stopping the story.

"Alice looked at the door with astonishment (that means she was surprised) and then she looked down at her feet."

You build the meaning right into the story without spoiling the fun of the story or the smooth flow of language.

After reading the story to your children, put the list of words you have chosen on the chalkboard. Don't pronounce them or teach them—just write them on the chalkboard.

Sit facing your children and say, "We are going to measure these words from the story to see if they sound like long words or short ones."

Put your hands together in clapping position and have your children do the same. Slowly move your hands apart as you say the first word on your list. You are showing the children the length of the word. Have them measure the word with their own hands as you say it. Then have them hold their hands in position while they go to the chalkboard and measure with their eyes which words says "astonishment."

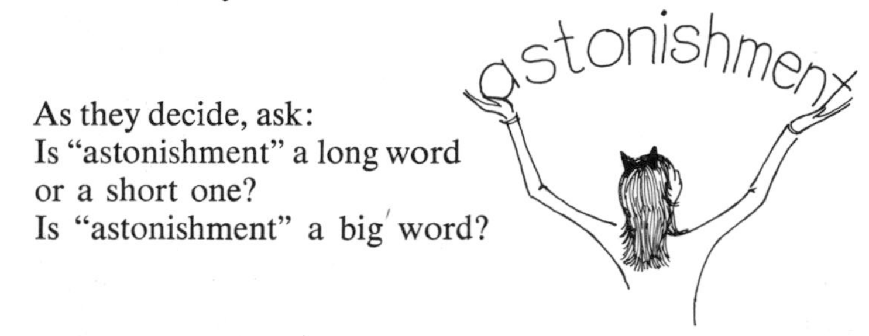

As they decide, ask:
Is "astonishment" a long word or a short one?
Is "astonishment" a big word?

When they find it, tell them they are wonderful to be able to find such a big word as "astonishment." And repeat: "Astonishment" means surprise.

After all the words have been measured, ask your children to find:

. . . the big word that means surprise,
. . . the little word that means to smile,
. . . the medium-sized word that means to think about something,
. . . the big word that means a strange place.

This work with words is planned to help your children:

1. Build their knowledge of the meanings of words.
2. Feel the size of words by the way they sound.

That is all it is intended to do. Don't teach the words, or try to get your children to sound them out, to remember them, or to spell them. If you do, you may gain a word but you will lose a skill.

Teaching Talk with Scribble Writing

While you are teaching your children to read, you can teach them to express their speech in writing. When they do this, they will be working with the raw materials of reading because that's what reading is—someone's ideas expressed in writing. Scribble stories, then, are a way of helping your children feel what it is like to talk on paper. Tell them you will draw a picture first to help them guess what you are going to talk about.

Sit beside a child while you do this. If you sit facing him he will see you writing from right to left.

Draw a simple picture
to illustrate
what you are going to write.

Then "write" your story, using a simple wavy line. Here is an example of a scribble story:

Notice that your "writing" starts with a big loop for capital letters and uses common punctuation marks. If your children ask you about these marks, tell them why you use them. Keep it simple. "This is a question mark. It tells that someone is asking a question. This is an exclamation mark. It tells that someone is angry."

Ask the children to look at your picture and see if they can guess what your story is about. This will teach them to use pictures as clues to the meaning.

Then "read" your scribble story to the children. In the illustration, the scribble story reads:

> Mom saw that Bill's cat was hungry.
> "Bill, did you feed your cat?" she asked.
> "Aw, Mom, I can't," Bill said. "I have to go play ball."
> "You feed that cat this instant!" Mom said.

Now it is the children's turn to write a scribble story to read to you. When they have finished, listen while they read their stories. Be liberal in your praise. It will be easy. Children write wonderful stories.

This is the time to put the typewriter to use. Have each child stand beside you and read his story while you type it out in words. Don't change anything. You want him to match what he says with words.

Put each typed story in a binder with the scribble story. Now each child has written his first book and he can read it.

Don't teach anything from his book. This is important. He can read it without any help from you.

Have the children do some scribble writing every day. On some days they may not want to write a scribble story. On these days, ask them three questions to which they know the answers and have them scribble the answers. Here are some examples of good questions:

1. What is your dog's name?

2. How old are you?

3. When do you go to bed?

4. What do you like most to eat?

5. What are the names of some television programs you like?

After you have read your three questions and they have scribbled their answers, ask the questions again and have the children read their answers.

Scribble writing helps a child learn that:

1. Marks on paper are talk written down.

2. Talk on paper goes from left to right.

Patterns in Sound

Words are made up of rhythmic patterns in sound. Help your children build skill in learning and using these sound patterns by playing a tapping game with them. Sit facing them and, with a pencil, tap out a simple pattern on the edge of the table. Have a child listen and then draw long and short marks on paper to show the pattern.

two long taps, one short — — -
two short taps, one long - - —
one short, one long, one short - — -

There are hundreds of variations of this you can use. Some children cannot do this at once. If a child lacks the necessary coordination, don't scold him or tell him he is wrong. Say, "That's fine," and keep on practicing until he can do it. Use only three taps at first. As the child gets good at imitating three taps, you can increase the number.

Remembering Ideas in the Proper Order: A Sequence Game

Your children need to learn to remember ideas in the proper order. This is a very important reading skill. Give them some practice with the following game:

1. Tell them you are going to ask them to do three things but that they must not start until you have said all three things:

   Put down your pencil.
   Stand by your chair.
   Scratch your head.

Now do them.

2. Tell them the next time they must do the three things in the order in which you say them:

   First, untie your shoe.
   Second, pick up your pencil.
   Third, hand me a book.

3. As the children learn to do this well, increase the number of things they are to do.

Perception of Patterns

There are many different types of patterns all around your children. Use these to help them learn about time and space and cabbages and kings.

1. Make a grocery list. Ask them, "Where would I find salt in the supermarket?"
   Draw a picture of the supermarket and let them help you list each item in the place where it is found.

2. Ask them questions about patterns.
   What is the very first thing you do when you get up in the morning? What do you do next? What is the first thing we do in school?

3. Play the "They both have" game with them. Ask such questions as "How are books and horses alike?" Each answer must start with, "They both have . . ." You can't see any ways that horses and books are alike? They both have eyes (i's). They both have backs. They both have tales. And in many other ways books and horses are alike. See how many you can think of.

4. Children walk many patterns each day. Draw maps to show:

   Where the rooms are in your house,
   Where the furniture is in a room,

   How to get
   to the grocery store,
   or the school,
   or any number
   of other places.

5. Take two words and ask, "How are these two words alike?" Perhaps they both start with the same letter. They both have other letters that are alike. They are both short. They both have letters.

The materials for playing this game are unlimited. You can use any questions that start "How are — like —?" Just fill in the blanks and you have ten minutes of fun that will improve a child's reading skills. You can use questions that involve what one does first, and what ones does after that. Use both kinds of questions. Each one builds an important thinking skill for reading.

Learning to Write the Letters

Letters link a child's speech to reading. The letters stand for the sounds he makes when he talks. If the child is to read as well as he talks, the letters of the alphabet need to be linked to the muscles of his body in every way possible. Learning to write the letters is one important way this is done. The simplest way to teach your children to write the letters is to use straight lines and circles. This is called manuscript writing. Since we will use the vowels first in teaching them to read, help them learn to write the vowels first.

a is written with a straight line
and a circle like this.
e is a straight line and a circle like this.
i is a straight line and a dot.
o is a circle.
u is a half circle and a straight line.

a
e
i
o
u

The consonants are made in the same way, with straight lines and circles. Have the children draw a straight line down the paper right in front of them. Have them show, with an outstretched hand, where the circle is in b, d, g, p.

Tell the child the straight line
is himself
and the circles or other lines
show where he puts things.
k, for example,
is the left arm and leg extended.

Have the children act this out
before they write it.

CHAPTER 3

Skill One: Knowing the Names of the Letters

Relating Letters to the Child's Body Imagery

Books contain letters that stand for the sounds of speech. This is the one thing about reading that is different from talking.

A child's first perceptual tool for reading is knowing the *names* of the letters. He already knows the sounds. He wouldn't be able to talk if he didn't. You can teach a child to read by teaching him to associate sounds with letters directly, but this is the hard way. We will use the easy, natural way.

A child learned the sounds that letters stand for through the muscles of his body, especially those of lip and tongue. This was the way he learned to talk. However, reading is listening to a book, not talking at it. So a child's reading must link lips, tongue, eyes, ears, hands, and every other muscle of his body to help him listen to the talk of books.

To teach them the names of the letters, *act them out.* Develop your own style and order. Your children will only be as interested as you appear to be.

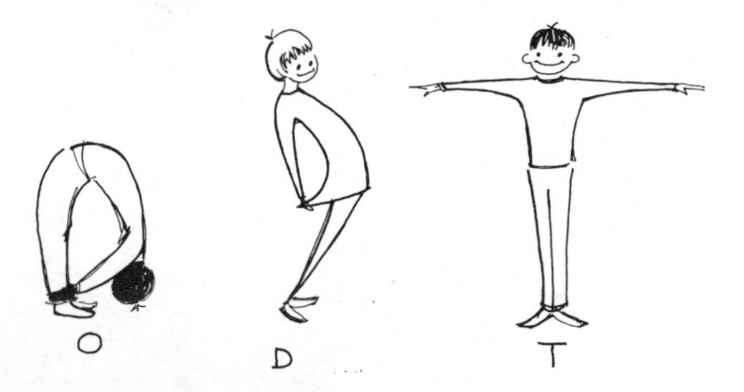

1. Bend over and take hold of your ankle and you are an O. Write the letter O on the board. Ask the children to be an O.

2. Stand straight and put out your stomach. You are a D.

Let the children decide how to act out the other letters. "Let's be a T," you say. Draw a large T on the blackboard. Stand up and extend your hands out from your body at shoulder height. Say to the children, "Now be a T."

3. Have them trace the T on the chalkboard with their finger. Keep telling them the name of the letter. Remember a child has to learn to hear a book.

Now the child's hand knows a T. His body knows a T. His ears know a T. Team all the ways of learning with a game everybody will enjoy. The game is called, "Let's see what we can make."

Take two large sheets of paper
on which you draw
two large letters T,
one on each sheet.

Show the children you can
make a table out of the T . . .

or a man wearing a hat . . .

or a Christmas tree.

Now take a red wax crayon and outline the T, so you can see it in the picture.

As you work, keep talking to the children about the T. You are training their ears.

Keep it fun. Everything a child does with books ought to be fun.

Go slowly. You are teaching the children something they will use all their lives. You want to do the job well. If they learn one letter each day, they will master the alphabet in less than one month. That's fast enough. There are other important things to do while they are learning the names of the letters.

Using the Everyday Environment

Build on his knowledge. Put to work what the children have learned. Call their attention to the letter every time you see it—or most of the time. Don't bore them and yourself by overdoing it.

Strike up the band when they find the letter and call your attention to it. This is wonderful. Now their eyes are learning to know the letter. A child will never forget the letters you teach him by building them into the muscles of his body. This is the way he learned to talk—and he doesn't forget how to talk, does he?

Reminders

1. Work for a short period and at the same time each day.

2. Be blind to everything a child does wrong.

3. See everything he does well and tell him you saw it.

CHAPTER 4

Skill Two: Knowing Where Sounds Are in Words

Locating Long Vowel Sounds in Words

Learning where sounds are in words is the second perceptual skill the children must learn in order to read. Be sure they know the names of most of the letters before you start this step.

The vowels a, e, i, o, u are the letters that give sound to words. A child is able to use vowel sounds at birth because he doesn't need to know how to control his lips and tongue to say them. When he substitutes vowel letters for the sounds, he will have difficulty if he can't find and feel these sounds. That is why being able to find a sound is an important perceptual skill in reading. We start with long vowel sounds since these are the *names* of the letters and the child has already learned them. Each step builds on an earlier one and utilizes the knowledge acquired previously.

This is how you can teach children to find sounds:

1. Start this step by having a child stand at the center of the chalkboard, so close to it that his nose touches the board. Put a large letter o in the spot where his nose touches the board when his head is level and his eyes are looking straight ahead.

2. Without shifting his position in any way, have him stretch out both arms at shoulder level. Put a large o at the fingertips of the left hand and another at the fingertips of the right hand.

3. Have the child stretch his hands out straight in front of him, stepping back as he does so, until the tips of his fingers are just touching the chalkboard.

4. In this lesson, use the child's dominant or preferred hand. He must not use both hands or shift from one hand to the other. Have him use the hand he uses to write his scribble stories. Have him extend this hand, with elbow straight, so that the hand points to the middle o. Say, "This o is in the middle." Point to the left and say, "This o is at the beginning." Point to the right and say, "This o is at the end."

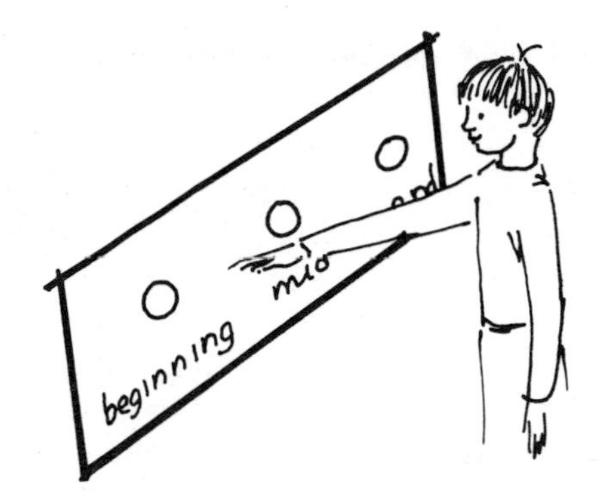

Continue this practice until the child points left when you say "beginning," right when you say "end," and center when you say "middle." Be sure he keeps his elbow straight. You want him to feel the pull of the directions in the muscles of his shoulder. Have the other children follow at their seats. If time permits, give each child an opportunity to do the lesson at the chalkboard.

5. Use the following list of words for this lesson:

boat	foam	load	piano	oats	over
banjo	bone	Ohio	open	so	loaf

For further practice, you may add other familiar words containing a long o. Do not allow them to say the word. The must show the position of the o by pointing with a straight arm to the proper letter on the chalkboard. Check by writing a word on the chalkboard and letting your children see that the o is not the beginning or ending sound. Use scribble writing for every letter except the one being found. For example, the o in boat is shown this way:

6. Use the other vowels e, i, a, and u in the same way. Here is a list of words to use. Add others as you wish.

beat read eat feed tea * three
see meat please Easter three

* If a child notices that the letter a is last in the word tea when you check it, tell him he is only finding letters he hears. Wc do not hcar thc lctter a in the word tea. Repeat the word while the child looks at it and let him check this for himself.

i

ice fire mice tire try idea

a

ate rake take ray bay lake

u

Utah tune use tube new mew

7. Have the children write the words in the word lists by using a combination of scribble writing and the vowels. Ask them to show you where the vowel is on the board before they write it. Use other words in the same way.

boat is written
load is written
oats is written
banjo is written
Ohio is written

Ask them to show you which word in their list says "boat." Which says "oats"? Which says "Ohio"? Use other words having the long sounds of e, i, a, and u in the same way.
As the children become proficient in finding the names or long vowel sounds in words, you can include words of several syllables in your "spelling tests." Potato is written 〰 o 〰 a 〰 o. Pronounce the word slowly, by syllables as the child writes it.

8. If the child does not add vowels to his scribble stories, you can now encourage him to do so. As you type his next scribble story, say, "I hear an *a* in *take*. It is in the middle. Show me the word *take* in your story. Let's put an *a* in the middle." Don't urge a child to take this step if he seems reluctant to do so. Keep helping him to find the *a, e, i, o,* and *u* and keep giving him "spelling tests." When he is ready, he will put the long vowels in his scribble stories. When he does, praise him for it. Not all stories need to be typed. You may do this with a small group one day. Another day, you may take another group. Thus, each child will have one or two of his stories typed for a class book. The children will begin to notice words with long vowel sounds in the spoken language heard daily. Call their attention to the *o* in *coke*. Ice cream has an i in the beginning. The service station is selling sn*o*w t*i*res. You will have many such opportunities to practice because the children's reading material is coming right out of their language.

   Go slowly. Nothing makes a child want to read as much as success in learning the skills.

CHAPTER 5

Skill Three: Naming the Long Vowels Heard in Words

Review

You are now ready for Skill Three in teaching children the perceptual skills for reading. Before you go to this step, be sure the children

1. Know the names of most of the letters

2. Can write the vowels, *a, e, i, o,* and *u.*

3. Can find the long vowel in words you say to them.

Being able to identify the letters he hears in words is an important reading skill for a child. It links what he says with what he sees in books. It also helps him to visualize a word he hears. If he can do this, he has a much better chance to remember words he hears people say and to recognize them when he sees them in reading.

Relating Vowels to Body Imagery Through the Use of Hands

Learning to shape vowels with the hands will help a child to get the feel of vowels. This is an important part of linking the muscles of the body to letters, just as in learning to talk he links the muscles of his body to sounds. Some suggested patterns for making the vowels with his hands are given here, but you may use other ways if your children find them easier. The important thing is that the child have in his hands a pattern that represents the form of the letter.

1. Put a large *a* on the chalkboard. Use a circle and a straight line. Tell your children you will make the *a* with your hands. Make a circle with your left hand and a straight line with your right hand. Hold your hands so the child is seeing the *a* in the correct position. Have your children make an *a* with their hands.

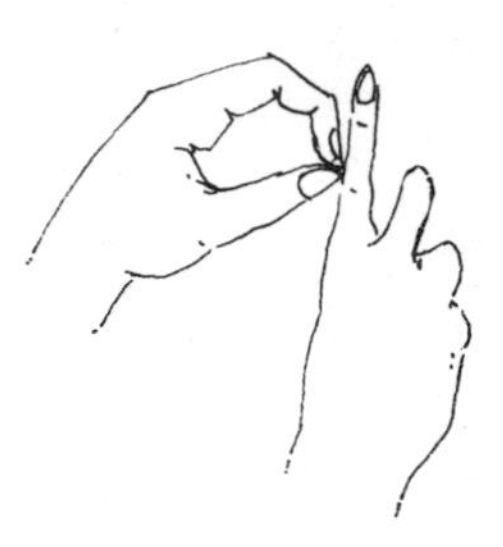

2. Make an *e*. First put it on the chalkboard. Then make a half-circle with your left hand, and use one finger of your right hand to complete the *e*. Have the children make the letter with their hands.

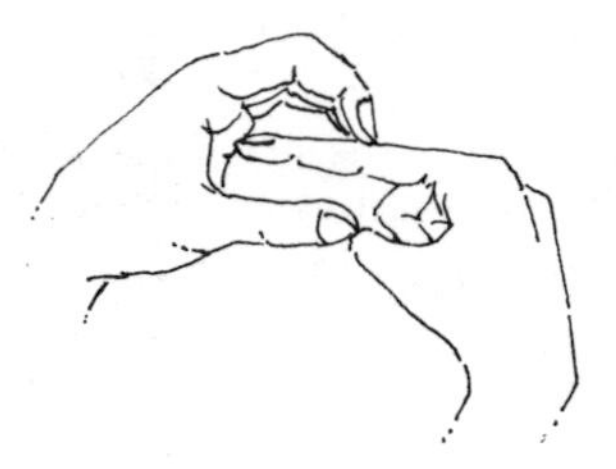

3. Make an *i*. Use one finger of the left hand for the straight line. Double up the fist of the right hand to make the dot.

4. The *o* is a circle with the left hand.

5. The *u* is a half-circle with the left hand.

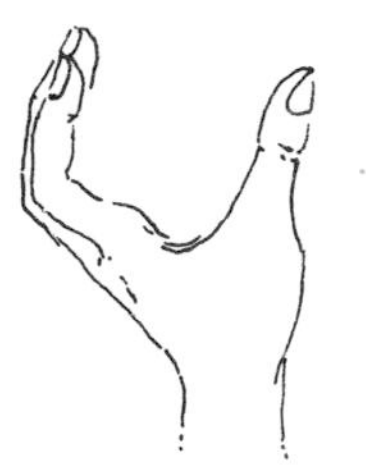

In making the *o* and *u*, the child may find it difficult to use his left hand alone if he is strongly right-handed. If he has difficulty, use the right hand for these letters.

Now practice having the children make the letters as you call them until they can make them quickly and easily. When they can do this, they are ready for the next part of this step.

Identifying Long Vowel Sounds in Words

Use the same words you used in Skill Two. Mix them up, so words having the same vowel sound do not come together. Say to the child, "Show me with your hands the letter you hear in *boat*."

Do not permit the child to say the word or the vowel. He must make it with his hands. If he shows any difficulty in making it, practice this with him until he is sure. If he is not sure which letter he hears in *boat,* go back and do some more practice on Skill Two. If a child is ready for a step, he ought to be able to do what is required of him with very little difficulty.

Writing Vowels that Are Heard

When the children can make the vowels correctly with their hands in words you say aloud to them, use this skill in writing. Say, "Show me the letters you hear in *boat*." When they have done this, tell them to write the word *boat*. Have them use a combination of scribble and the vowel. They will use a scribble for the *b,* an *o* for the vowel, and a scribble for the *t*. Since the *a* in boat is not heard, it is ignored at this time. Use all the other words from your word lists at this time and in this way. Add interesting new words you and your children have heard.

This is an important exercise in this skill, but it is built on the two earlier exercises and should not be used until the child does the first two very well. Proceed in this way:

1. Say a word from your list. Have the children make the vowel with their hands.

2. Have the children write the word as in Skill Two.

3. Write the word on the chalkboard and have them check it as *you* say it aloud. *Do not ask the children to say it. You are teaching them to listen to words.*

Listening to Vowels in Words Heard During the Day

At any time during the day you and your children are doing things together, you will hear words with long vowel sounds. Discover them together. Add them to your list, using a combination of scribble writing and the vowel. Perhaps your children can keep a little notebook in which they list these words. *Do not ask them to identify the other letters at this time.*

Take plenty of time to let your children master Skill Three. There are many other things you can be doing with them while they are doing so. If you are tempted to rush the steps in the teaching, go back to Chapter Two and select some of these activities to round out your teaching time with your children. All of these exercises are important phases in teaching a child to read.

In addition to those things suggested in Chapter Two, play other games with your children to help them develop the use of their bodies. Any game that uses both eyes, or both hands, or both feet will help a child become a good reader.

CHAPTER 6

Skill Four; Counting the Sounds in a Word

Relationship of This Skill to Reading and Talking

Most people are aware today that there is a vast universe of space outside our planet. Few people, however, ever think that there is a world of space surrounding language. We use this space factor physically when we learn to talk. There is rhythm to talking. Some people talk very rapidly and others drawl. This is a matter of distance between words, or the extent to which we hang onto a sound before we go to the next one. Much has been written about the space of language but this is not important to teaching a child to read. It is only important that we know that space is a very vital part of language and that a child will use this space to learn to read just as he used it to learn to talk.

At school age, a child already knows and uses the space of talk. You will use that knowledge in Skill Four to help him learn the space of written language by having him count the number of things he hears in words.

The goal of this exercise is to help children become aware that there are a number of things to be heard on each side of the vowel in words. You have taught them to start with the vowel in looking at a word or in listening to it. Continue doing that. Before you start, it is important for you to know that accuracy in counting the number of things heard is not important. Knowing that there are a number of things to hear is important. With this in mind, you are ready to start.

Finding the Number of Sounds in a Word

1. Sit across the table from your children. Tell them you are going to count the number of things they hear in words as you say them aloud. Do not let the children see the words. You want to train their ears to hear the separate sounds in a word. First ask them, "What letter do you hear in *boat*?" Have them *show* you by making the *o* with their hands. Do not permit them to use their mouths to respond. Reading is listening to books talk to you.

2. Ask your children, "Where is the *o* in *boat*?" Have them show you with their writing hand as they learned to do in Skill Three.

3. Ask the children, "How many things do you hear in *boat*?" At this point you must use your own language space a little. Imagine that your children have written the word *boat* on the table in front of them. Keep this in mind when showing them the number of things heard in the word. Use their left and their right. Ask the children to put up the number of fingers that show how many things they hear in the word *boat*.

4. Now show them how many things are to be heard in *boat*. Put your elbow on the table. Keep in mind the word that would be on the paper in front of your children, and use their left for beginning. Say, "Let's see if you are right."

With the back of your hand to your children and your fist closed, say "o" and put up a middle finger.

Say "bo" and put up a finger in front of the "o" finger and to the children's left. Now say "boat" and put up a finger to the right of the "o."

Remember this is to the child's right.

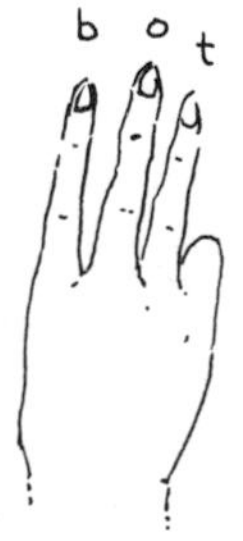

b o t

You'll feel more secure with this step if you practice a little alone before trying to teach it. Remember, no consonant is said alone. Always start with the vowel and add the consonant to it. This is exactly the way the child learned to talk. He started with the vowels and added the consonant as he learned to make his lips and tongue do what he wanted them to do. To teach this step, use words from the word list you used to teach the children long vowel sounds.

Here are some examples you can use to check yourself:

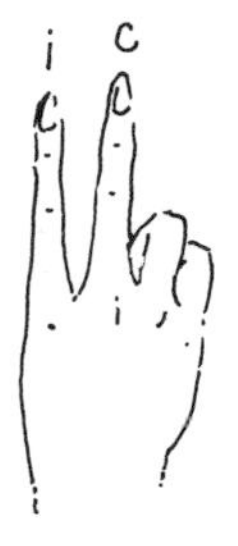

ice

What letter do you hear? (i)
Where is the i? (beginning)
How many things do you hear?
(One finger for i, another to the child's right as you say "ice")
Remember you do not hear the e in *ice*.

snow

What letter do you hear? (o)
what is the o? (ending)
How many things do you hear? (One finger for o, a finger to the child's left as you say "no," two fingers to the left of the o finger as you say "snow")

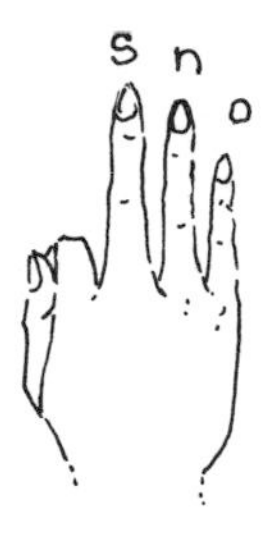

Later you may want to use words of more than one syllable. When you do, treat each syllable as if it were a single word.

CHAPTER 7

Skill Five: Associating Long Vowel Sounds with Consonants

Review

When you are ready for this step in the reading lessons, your children will be able to tackle the job of working with the actual reading of syllables. It is very important that these efforts be successful in order that your children may have the confidence that is needed for enjoyment of reading. Before you undertake this part of the instruction, check them on the skills you have already taught them:

1. Do they know the names of the letters?

2. Can they write the letters, using lines and circles?

3. Can they find the long vowel sounds in words spoken to them?

4. Can they name the vowels in words spoken to them?

5. Can they count the number of sounds they hear in words spoken to them?

6. Have they written several scribble stories?

If the answer to these six questions is "yes," you are ready for the next step. If the answer is "no," keep on working on the steps which are answered "no." Continue to work on the activities described in Chapter Two.

Relating the Letter B to the Long Vowel Sounds

Having mastered the first four steps in learning to read, your children are now ready to be taught to combine long vowel sounds with other letters to make open syllables. This is the way you will teach them these skills:

1. Put the letter b on the chalkboard. Ask the child to show you where the e is in be.

2. Write another letter b under the first one. Ask the children to show you where the a is in ba. Do the same thing with the vowels i, o, and u. Be careful always to say the consonant with the vowel. For example, there is no e in bo. You do not say "beo." When a consonant is combined with a vowel, the name of the consonant changes to conform with the vowel sound. This is the only unusual thing about this step, but it should not be difficult for your children to grasp.
   All consonants are syllables to begin with. When you say the names of consonants, you say a syllable. Here are some examples: be, ce, de, ef, ka. Say the names of the other consonants and you will see that all consonants are spoken by a lip and tongue position combined with either a long or short vowel. This is why it is so important for your children to learn the names of the letters. They already know the syllables that make up words in reading. They learned them as they learned to talk, by saying vowels and then adding consonants to them. We will use the names of the consonants to link what is printed on paper with their talk.

3. You now have on the chalkboard a list of syllables:

   be
   ba
   bi
   bo
   bu

   Now tell the children that these are syllables, or parts of words. And put a scribble after each syllable to show that it is only part of a word.

Using the Syllables as Context Clues to Words

1. You are now ready to use these syllables as context clues to words as your children will do when they actually read books. A context clue is something you use with the other meanings in a sentence to help you guess a new word. For example, in the sentence, "We are going to take the bo . . . to go fishing," you know that the bo does not stand for fishing line and it does not stand for bait. Why? Because of a combination of the way the word starts and the meaning of the sentence. This is what is meant by context clues. Say to the children, "I am going to write a story about boats. Which word would I write to say 'boats'? The word 'boats' starts with 'bo.' " Let the children show you how the word should start by pointing to the syllable bo. Use the other syllables in the same way. For example, "I hope the fish will bite. Which syllable would I use to start the word 'bite'? It starts 'bi.' "

2. Give the children a "spelling test." Dictate words and have them scribble to show the rest of the word. Some good words to use are:

   baby bike bugle beat bone

   You will be able to think of many others.

3. Encourage the child to put in the syllables in his scribble stories by calling his attention to them when he reads his story aloud to you and you type it. Do this in the same way you did for vowel sounds.

The Relationship of Other Consonants to Long Vowel Sounds

Teach the other consonants that say their names by a combination of long vowels and the consonant. These letters are *b, d, j, k, p, t, v, z*. You will note that *c, g, h,* and *q* have not been included because these consonants represent a variable sound. It is better for your children to deal with consistent and predictable situations when they are learning a new skill. They can deal with the variations after they have learned the skill. One does not ask a new driver to deal with complicated traffic problems.

Take plenty of time with this step and enjoy it. When your children find out about syllables and learn to use them to identify new words, they are learning one of the most important reading skills they will ever learn. There are words all around your children that use these beginning syllables. At the service station, you will buy a new t*u*be for your t*i*re. At the drug store, you will get some tooth p*a*ste. Call the children's attention to these words. When you read stories to them and list words for them to measure (see Chapter Two), notice those words that start with these syllables. They are called "open syllables" because they end with vowel sounds. But you need not teach this to the children at this time. After all, the teacher needs to know a little more than his pupil.

CHAPTER 8

Skill Six: Knowing Short Vowel Sounds

Review

The children are ready to learn the space of short vowel sounds as they are used in reading after they are able to:

1. Name the letters of the alphabet as they see them on paper.
2. Write the letters using lines and circles.
3. Find long vowel sounds in words spoken to them.
4. Name the long vowel sounds heard in words spoken to them.
5. Count the number of sounds heard in words containing long sounds.
6. Write scribble stories and words.
7. Read open syllables containing long vowel sounds, and the consonants *b, d, j, k, p, t, v,* and *z.*

You know how important it is for your children to master each skill before they go on to the next one. Go slowly and keep their work interesting at each step by including some of the activities given in Chapter Two in each lesson.

Two Important Ideas

The short vowel sounds are no more difficult to teach than the long vowel sounds, and you already know how easy that was. Before we start on this skill, there are two important ideas for you to keep in mind as you teach:

1. The child doesn't need to say the short vowel sounds, for he has been saying them ever since he was born. He needs to associate the short vowel sound with the letter that stands for it, and he needs to know when the vowel is long and when it is short.

2. Do not teach a child that o says "ah." In other words, do not associate the name of the vowel with the short sound it has in words. This is a wasteful and unnecessary step and will keep a child from getting a quick, clear sound of a word. You will teach him to recognize when the letter o stands for a long sound and when it stands for a short sound by a syllable pattern. But more about that later. Right now you are going to teach him to associate the short vowel with the letter that stands for it in reading. You are going to say "ah" and use the letter o to signal this sound without calling the letter o.

Employing Earlier Skills to Learn About Short Vowel Sounds

In previous skills, the children have learned how to find, recognize, and count sounds in words. We will now employ these same techniques in teaching the short vowel sounds. Instead of asking the children where the "a" is in *a*te, you will ask them where the "a" is in *a*t.

Go back and review Skills Two, Three, and Four. Now follow these procedures again with your children. Only this time use vowel sounds (the short ones) instead of vowel names (the long ones). Everything else is exactly the same.

Here are some lists of words to get you started on teaching the short vowel sounds. Add any others you wish.

a as in *at*

answer, am, cat, jam, after, at, camp, trap, ran, Jack

e as in *edge*

enter, net, left, elephant, get, jello, men, ten, fence

i as in *in*

in, intent, pin, lift, mint, since, kindle, dinner, fin

o as in *on*

on, often, got, fox, moss, jog, log, lost, onward, onto

u as in *under*

under, us, just, must, rust, tusk, mud, muscle, fuss, unto

Utilizing Body Imagery to Learn Short Vowel Sounds

You are now going to play a game with your children. This is a most serious game in spite of the fact that it will be lots of fun. It combines all the child's learning to help him know the short vowel sounds so well that he will never forget them. This is the way to play the game:

1. Sit beside the children and write a scribble story you will read to them.

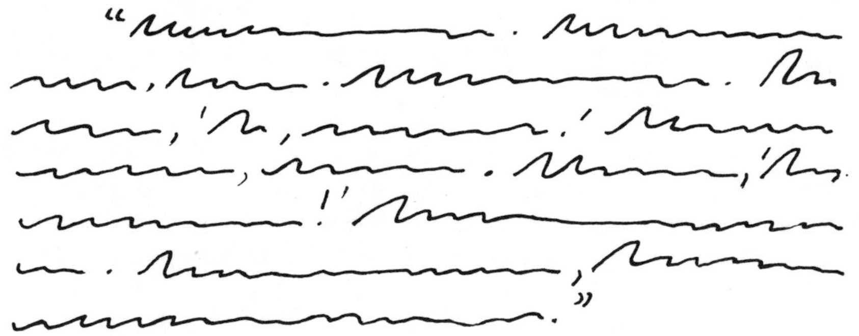

The hero of your story will be Ed (for boys) or Edna (for girls).

2. Read your scribble story to your children. It goes this way:

"Ed (or Edna) went to school. When he got to the door of his room, he didn't go in. He just stood there. The teacher said, 'Ed, go sit in your chair.' Did Ed obey his teacher? No, Ed wanted to play. So he stood at his chair. Then he got on his chair, and under his chair. The teacher said, 'Ed, get in your chair this instant!' So Ed got in his chair but only on the very edge of it. When the teacher looked angry, Ed sat way back in his chair and he sat up very straight."

3. Now say to the children, "You be Ed (Edna) and when I read the part of the story that says Ed stood at the chair, you stand at your chair." Read the scribble story again and wait for the children to act out the directions.

4. To develop this skill, use the directions only. Say, "Stand at your chair," and wait for your children to stand at their chairs. Say, "Get under your chair. Get on your chair. Get on the edge of your chair. Sit in your chair."

5. Repeat the directions, but this time use only the signal words, *on, in, edge, at, under*. If your children show any hesitation, go back and work with step 4 until they do it easily, and then drop all words except the direction words. When they can follow the direction words quickly and easily, you are ready for step 6.

6. This time you will give the vowel sounds only, and your children will act out the word represented. Say, "Stand 'a' your chair," and wait for the children to stand *at* their chairs. Be sure you use the short vowel sound rather than the name of the letter. Use the other short vowel sounds in the same way. Say "i" and wait for them to sit *in* their chairs, "o" and wait for them to stand *on* their chairs, "u" and wait for them to get *under* the chairs, "e" and wait for them to get on the *edges* of the chairs. If a child has difficulty responding to the sounds only, go back and practice step 5 some more.

7. Next use hand signals with your voice to help the children associate the form of the letter with its short sound. Make an o with your hands and say the short sound "o." Wait for the children to get *on* their chairs. Do the same thing with each of the other vowel sounds. Make the vowel with your hand as you say its short sound, and wait for the children to act out the word represented.

8. This time you will use the hand signals only. If the children have mastered the preceding steps, they will "hear" the vowel sound as you give the hand signal only. Again they will act it out in response to your hand signal.

If they hesitate, appear confused, or act out the wrong word, say the sound immediately and give the hand signal with it. Wait for them to act it out. Continue with this step until the children can act out each word as you give the hand signal only.

9. Now say the short vowel sound, giving the hand signal as you say it. Have the children give the hand signal as they act out the directions. For example, you will say "o" and make an o with your hand. The children will get *on* their chairs and make an o with their hands. Do not permit them to say "on." You are teaching them to associate short vowel sounds with the letters that represent them. They have been saying short vowel sounds since they were born, so they don't need to learn to do that. They need to learn to *hear* the sounds letters represent.

10. Now the children are ready to put their talk into actual words because you have linked the form of the letters representing the vowels to the sound through the muscles of their bodies. Draw five chairs on the chalkboard.

Ask a child to show where the "a" is in *at*. Be sure to use the short sound and not the name of the letter a. The child will point to the left with his elbow straight, as you have taught him to do. Write the word *at* under the first chair and draw a boy (or girl) standing at the chair.

Ask the child to show you where the "o" is in *on*. Write "on" under the second chair on the chalkboard. Draw a child on the chair.

Ask him to show you where the "u" is in *under*. Write "under" below the third chair and draw a child under the chair. (Since most school chairs are too small for a child to get under, let them squat beside their chairs.)

Ask him where the "e" is in *edge*. Write "edge" under the fourth chair. Draw a child sitting on the edge of the chair.

Ask him where the "i" is in *in*. Write the word "in" below the fifth chair. Draw a child in the chair.

Now say to the child, "Get 'o' your chair" (short sound of o) and make the vowel with your hand. When he is on his chair, have him make the sound with his hand. Now erase the *on* from under the chair on the chalkboard and write just the letter o.

Do the same with all the other short vowel sounds. Say the sound, show it with your hand, have the child act it out and show it. Then erase the word from under the chair and substitute the letter that indicates the sound. The child now has a vowel sound dictionary that is keyed to his ears and the muscles of his body. It is a *talk-to-reading* vowel sound dictionary.

Now get the children started using these short vowel sounds in their scribble writing. Have them draw five chairs on a sheet of paper. Tell them you will play the "x marks the spot" game. You want them to put an x on each chair where Ed (or Edna) is when you tell them. Say, "Ed is 'o' (short vowel sound) his chair." Wait for the children to put an x on their first chair. Then point to the correct chair on the chalkboard and say again, "Ed is 'o' his chair." If the children put the x in the wrong place, say nothing. They will learn. If they put it in the correct place, be lavish in your praises. Do the same thing with the other vowel sounds. If a child continues to put the x in the wrong place, it only means he needs further practice in steps 3 to 10.

Give the children a spelling test using the short vowel sounds. Use the words from your short vowel list (see Skill Six: *Knowing the Short Vowel Sounds*). You may, of course, add other words to this list as the children become skilled at identification of short vowel sounds. First, establish the children's space for the word to be spelled by asking them: "Where is the 'o' (short sound) in 'got'?" "What letter says its sound in 'got'?" (The child makes an o with his hands.) "How many things are in 'got'?" (He holds up the correct number of fingers.) Watch the children do this. If you have taught them well, they will put up a finger for the o, then one to the left for *go,* and finally one to the right for *got*. If they do not do this, review the step with short vowel sounds.

Now ask the children to write *got*. They will use a combination of scribble and the letter o.

Do the same thing with the other words from the short vowel list.

Again, you should encourage the children to put the short vowel sounds in their scribble writing by calling their attention to them as you type the stories for their books. They should have quite a collection of stories by this time. These stories build language flow so the pattern of a child's talk flows smoothly onto paper. Therefore, do not put too much stress upon their writing in the short vowel sounds as they write their scribble stories. Just call their attention to two or three words after the story is written and as you type it for the book of stories.

When a child goes to the drug store, he can add *drug* to the list of words in his notebook. Let a child put down what he hears in his word notebook. Don't insist that he put down what you see. Children do not learn in the same way as adults. You are inclined to see or visualize a word you hear. A child hears and translates this into the muscles of his body by writing. You spell a word. A child puts it down in sounds. For example, you would spell the word candy. A child will write [illegible] a [illegible] i because that is the way he says it. That is good. He will learn that we do not always spell a word the way we say it.

So help the children add words they hear all around them to the word notebook. If you observe what he puts down, you will know where he needs further practice.

CHAPTER 9

Skill Seven: Relating Short Vowel Sounds to Consonants

General Review of Readiness

Very soon now your children will be independent readers. This is a very exciting thing to watch. Don't spoil the good work you have done up to this point by rushing the next skill. Check your children carefully before proceeding.

1. Do they know the names of all the letters?
2. Can they write the letters using lines and circles?
3. Can they find the long vowel sounds in words spoken aloud to them?
4. Can they name the long vowel sounds heard in words said to them aloud?
5. Can they count the number of sounds heard in words having long vowel sounds?
6. Can they do with short vowel sounds the same things they do with long vowels in 3, 4, and 5?
7. Do they associate short vowel sounds with the letters that stand for them?
8. Have they had many experiences writing scribble stories and words?

If the answer to any of these questions is "no," review that skill before going on to Skill Seven.

If the answer to question 1 is "no," go back to chapter Three. Find out exactly which letters the child does not know.

Test him by typing out a list of letters and asking him to name each one as you point to it. Be sure the letters are mixed up. A child can say, "a, b, c, d, e, f, g" in order without knowing the names of any of those letters. Teach the letters the child does not know, using the suggestions in Chapter Three. From now on, the child needs to know the names of all the letters.

If the answer to question 2 is "no," go back to Chapter Two and review the directions for teaching a child to write the letters. He should be able to write most of the letters before he goes on to Skill Seven.

If the answer to question 3 is "no," give further practice on this step, using the suggestions given in Chapter Four.

Chapter Five tells you how to teach a child the name the vowels have in words. If the answer to question 4 is "no," go back to this chapter and give the child further practice on this skill.

Chapter Six is the one you will use if the answer to question 5 is "no."

If a child has difficulty with finding, naming, or counting with short vowel sounds (question 6), you should review the activities suggested in Chapter Eight.

The child should have written at least ten scribble stories before he is ready to go on to Skill Seven. Scribble stories aren't just fun exercises. They are a vital part of helping a child use his ability to talk in learning to read.

Continue to use some of the activities suggested in Chapter Two in every reading lesson. Each of these suggestions is designed to strengthen an important perceptual skill for reading and to help children enjoy reading.

Finally, it's a good idea to use and review all the six skills your children have learned. They will not forget them, because each skill has been built into the muscles and the child takes his reading skills with him everywhere he goes. He practices his reading skills every time he says anything, every time he hears sounds as people talk, and every time he sees anything. The child's reading skills aren't in a book. They are in him. They are helping him express himself, develop his personality, get the things he wants out of life. They are tools and he needs to use each one well.

So review all the steps whenever the opportunity arises. Let your children know the joy of doing things they can do well.

Relating the Letter F and the Other Consonants to the Short Vowel Sounds

In this skill you will teach the children to relate short vowel sounds to the names of the letters in exactly the same way you taught them to relate long vowel sounds to the names of letters. But this time you will use the consonants that have short vowel sounds in their names. These consonants are f, l, m, n, r, s, and x. Can you hear the vowel sounds when you say the names of these letters? If you wrote down everything you heard, it would look like this: *ef, el, em, en, or, es,* and *eks.* All right? Suppose we start with the letter f.

1. Ask the children to show you with their hands where they hear the "e" in *ef.* Be sure you use the short vowel sound.

2. Write the letter *f* on the chalkboard. But the *e* where it belongs to the left of the consonant. Put a scribble to the right so the "word" looks like this: ef ~~~

3. Put another *f* on the chalkboard. Ask the children to show you with their hands which letter to write first to say "if." If the children hesitate, say, "Ed is *in* the chair. 'i.' "

4. Do the same thing with the other short vowel sounds.

5. You now have this list of syllables on the chalkboard:

   ef
   if
   of
   af
   uf

6. Ask a child to show you, by pointing to it, which syllable says if, of, ef, uf. Ask him which syllable you would write first if you wanted to write effort, after, off, offer, afternoon.

7. Repeat this procedure (1-6) with the consonants *l, m, n, s.* Do not use the consonants *r* and *x* at this time.

Again you can use these syllables in scribble writing by calling a child's attention to them as you type his story. Do not urge him too much on the use of vowel sounds in his story. The most important thing he gains from writing scribble stories is the joy of expressing his talk on paper.

Using the Syllables as Context Clues to Words

Context clues can be utilized with good results now and will motivate the child in his first free writing experiences. Context clues are introduced as follows: As you write on the board, say, "You know this letter's name (write b). How many things do you hear when you say b? You hear the e say its name. Where is the e? Let's put the e last because that's where we hear it. (Write be.) Suppose I wanted to write about a boat. How would I start it? Where is the o in boat? Let's put that on the board." Write bo.

Proceed in the same way to establish the concept of the open syllables of *bi, ba, bu*. Then say to the children, "These are only parts of a word. Let's put a line after each one to show that there is more to the word." The open syllables on the board will appear this way:

be bi bu
ba bo

"Now we are ready for some fun! I am going to say something but I will need someone to finish what I am going to say. You find the part of a word that will help me finish what I am going to say. My dog wants a . . ." The children suggest *bone*. You then ask, "What part of a word would I need to write the 'bo' in bone?" The children find the correct syllable on the board.

Later on the children can write these responses and tell what they think you need to finish the syllable, and what syllable they would choose to finish the sentence. With a little practice, they will begin to write sentences of their own and even stories. They will use beginning syllables and a line to indicate the rest of the word. Obviously they will not develop unusual proficiency in this writing until the vowel sounds (short vowels) have been introduced.

CHAPTER 10

Skill Eight: Knowing About the Syllables in a Word

Review

This is the final skill in mastering the perceptual skills involved in learning the mechanics of reading. When a child has mastered this skill, he will be able to read anything he can say. That does not mean a primer or a first reader. It means anything he can say when he talks. From this point on, a child's reading will be limited only by his vocabulary.

You know by now that you should not start this skill until your children have mastered all the steps that came before. Go back to the beginning of Chapter Nine and check them on all the skills reviewed there. Then check them on the skills in Step Seven.

Body Imagery to Help Determine the Sound of the Vowel in a Syllable

In this step you will use the space skills the child learned when he found long and short vowel sounds by showing where they were with his hands. This is what you will do:

1. Seat your children in front of the chalkboard. You write on the chalkboard: be, eb, de, ed, fe, ef, te, et, se, es, pe, ep. Say the syllables aloud as you write them. You will notice there is a pattern to these syllables. Each uses the vowel e. The vowel changes from long to short as it is moved from one side of the consonant to the other. That is what you want the children to learn. But you are not going to tell them. You are going to have them experience it in the muscles of their bodies.

2. Now erase the syllables you have written, and write them again, one pair at a time. Write *be* and have a child show with his writing hand where the e is in be. Now write *eb* and have him show you where the e is. Be sure to use the short vowel sound this time and not the name of the letter. You want the child to think the short sound when he sees a vowel to the left of the consonant and the long sound when he sees a vowel to the right of the consonant. This is an important skill in reading.

Now use the next pair of syllables in the same way. Do not ask the children to say these syllables. They can already do that for they have learned to hear them and to feel the pattern in the muscles of their bodies.

3. When the children can shift their hand easily from right to left when you write and say the syllable pair *be, eb,* and the others you have used, you will have them write them as you say them. In this exercise, you will not write the syllables on the chalkboard. You will merely say them. Have the children show where the vowel is with their hands and then write it on paper. They are to remain seated while they do this. It will not be as effective for the children to write the syllables on the chalkboard.

   Be sure the child keeps his arm straight as he shows you where the vowel is. You want him to feel the pull of direction in his shoulders. Use all the syllable pairs in this way, first having the child show you where the vowel is and then writing it on paper in front of him. Do not use other vowels yet. Use only the long and short sounds of e. The child is learning a pattern of the position of the vowel in relation to the consonant.

4. When the child can write the syllables with the long and short sounds of e quickly and accurately, use other

vowels in the same way. With each vowel repeat exercises 1 to 3, giving your children plenty of time. They should do each new thing required of them quite easily. If you have difficulty, you are rushing a skill. Go back and review the vowel sounds. Play the "Ed" game with them every day.

Developing the Ability to See the Visual Pattern of Syllables in a Word

When you went to grade school, your teacher probably taught you to divide words into syllables—with a long set of rules. Your children are more fortunate because you will have to teach them only one rule. This is the place where you will train their eyes to see what they already know. From the moment your children learned the name of the first letter, they have been working with syllables, because the name of every consonant in our language is a syllable. You have only to apply this knowledge of what the child sees in a word through the perceptual skills he has been taught.

Do it this way:

1. Ask the children to show you with their hands where the "e" is in *be.*
2. Write *be* on the chalkboard.
3. Ask the children to show you with their hands where the a is in *ba.*
4. Write *ba* on the chalkboard right beside *be*. It will look like this: *beba.*
5. Tell your children you will put the *ba* first and make a word. Write *babe* (baby) on the chalkboard. Ask your children to listen and see if they hear a word. "It means a small person."
6. Ask the children to show you with their hands where the o is in *bo.*
7. Add *bo to babe*. Your word now looks like this: *babebo.*

8. Tell the children you have now made a new word. Ask them to listen while you read it. Read the three syllables as though they were an actual word. Do not ask the children to say it.

9. Ask the children to show you with their hands where the *be* is (beginning); where the *bo* is (ending).

10. Tell them you will say the "word," only this time you will say part of it wrong. Ask them to tell you which part is wrong. Read aloud *bebabo* and wait for a child to tell you the first part is wrong. Do the same thing with other parts of the word. Do not make more than one syllable wrong at the same time.

11. Now erase the "word." Dictate it to your children in syllables and have them write the "word."

12. Make other words in the same way. Always start by asking the children to show you with their hands where the vowel is. Here is an exercise for you to practice on:
    a. Where is the e in *le?* Show me with your hand. (Write le on the chalkboard as they show you.)
    b. Where is the a in *sa*? (Write sa under the first syllable.)
    c. Where is the i in *ti*? (Write ti under the second syllable.)
    d. Now I will make a word. (Write *lesati* on the chalkboard.)

    Use this new word as you did in steps 8, 9, 10, and 11.

13. Now do the same thing with short vowel sounds. Use only syllables having the short vowel sound in the middle.

    Here is an exercise for you to practice on:
    a. Where is the o in *bos*? Show me with your hand. (Be sure to use the short vowel sound as in *on*. Write bos on the chalkboard.)
    b. Where is the a in *bas*? Show me with your hand. (Write bas on the chalkboard under the first syllable.)
    c. Where is the i in *bis*? Show me with your hand. (Write bis under the second syllable.)

d. Now I will take these three parts and make a word. (Write *besbasbis* on the chalkboard.)
e. Use this word as you did in long vowels in steps 8, 9, 10, and 11. If your children have difficulty with these syllables containing short vowel sounds, go back to the very first thing you did with short vowel sounds and review every exercise.

Take plenty of time with this exercise. Use many "words" and take all the steps. Do not skip any of them. Each exercise develops a specific skill for reading and helps the children with the next exercise. Here is a list of "words" to use for practice:

taftiltos
mismulmab
salsussif

Do you see the pattern? Fine. You will be able to make up other words for practice. It is best not to use "real" words at this time. You are not teaching your children a word. You are teaching them a perceptual skill.

The One Rule for Syllables

You are now ready to teach your children the only rule they will need in order to read any word they can say. You will teach them always to look ahead in a word to the very first letter after the first vowel. This letter will tell them if the vowel is long and says its name, or short and says its sound. Let's see how this works.

Potato

The first letter after the first vowel is t. Does the t stay with the o or move on to the right? *It moves on to the right whenever it is followed by a vowel.*

That means that the first syllable is either *po* or *op*. Your children already know these patterns. They know that a vowel to the right of a consonant says its long sound or name; that a vowel to the left of a consonant says its short sound. The first syllable in the word potato is *po*—because the t went on. So you say the name of the o, or its long sound.

Now do the same thing with the second syllable. There is a t after the a, but it goes on because it is followed by a vowel.

So you have *ta* as the second syllable. Is it *ta* or *at*? Do you see how your children are using the skill you taught them after you played the *be-eb, le-el, fe-ef* game?

The last syllable in potato is, of course, *to*. Is it *to* or *ot*?

As you can see, if you have taught the preceding skills well, your children now have only one rule to learn to read a word: that the consonant following a vowel determines the sound of the vowel by going on if it is followed by a vowel—or coming back if it is followed by a consonant. If it goes on to the right, the vowel sound is long. If it comes back to the left, the vowel sound is short. Do you remember how it was in be-eb?

"But," you will say, "there are exceptions. How about in . . .?"

Stop right there. When you teach a person to drive a car, you teach him how to handle the car. Then you teach him what to do in an emergency. A phonetic rule isn't intended to deal with all the problems of pronunciation. No rule can, because pronunciation is determined by usage. Our language grows and changes all the time. A child does not have to have an accurate pronunciation of a word to remember it. He does have to have a feeling for the word, a perceptual link that is related to his speech. If you listen to him talk, you will see that he always starts a syllable with a consonant if that is possible. This is so he can "wrap his tongue" around the syllable and get the feel of it.

Made-up Words in Teaching Syllables

Since we want to teach the child how syllables are made, you will use "made-up" words, rather than "real" ones. In that way, a child does not have to deal with exceptions while he is learning the pattern. He does not have to deal with unexpected emergencies while he is learning where the gear shift is on the car.

You already know how to teach him to read the syllables in a word, don't you? This, then, is a review of how to do it:

1. Write a "made-up" word on the chalkboard. A made-up word is just an assortment of syllables of two and three letters. *to* is a two letter syllable; *tos* is three letters.

That's easy, isn't it? Suppose you start by writing this word on the chalkboard:

tolastos

Tell your children you will show them how to hear this new word.

2. Ask them: "What is the name of the first vowel? Which letter comes right after this vowel? Which letter comes next?"

3. Now tell your children that the l will go this way (point to the child's right) because it sees another vowel ahead. So the *to* is left behind, and it is the very first part of the new word.

4. Now write *to* and *ot* on the chalkboard. Ask your children to show you where the o is in *to*; where the o (short sound) is in *ot*. Then ask them, "Does the first part of the new word say *to* or *ot*. If your children find this difficult, you need to go back and work on Skill Eight. The perceptual skill is the backbone of all syllabication.

5. Ask your children to find the next vowel. It is the a. Which letter follows the a? Which letter is after the s? Tell your children that the s will come back (point to the child's left) since it does not see a vowel ahead of it. It sees only a t. When the s comes back, does it talk with with the vowel this way—*sa*—or this way—*as*? It says *as,* and don't forget the l came to the a, so all of it says *las*. This is the second part of the word.

6. Do exactly the same thing with the third syllable. In this syllable the letter s comes back because there aren't any more letters for it to go with.

7. Tell your children you will say the new word two or three times and they are to listen. Say the word in syllables.

8. Read the word this way: *to mas tos*. Ask a child which part was wrong. (He is to show you with his hand if it is the beginning, middle, or end.) Now read the word: *to las ros*. Have the child show which part is wrong. Now read it *mos las tos*. Have the child show which part is wrong.

9. Tell the children you want them to give you a test. Provide each child with a sheet of paper with the numbers 1 to 10 written in a column. Tell your children you will answer ten questions about the word. They are to put an x by the number of every question you get wrong. Here is the test:

   a. The first part of the word is *to* (long vowel)
   b. The middle part of the word is *las* (short vowel)
   c. The end of the word is *tos* (short vowel)
   d. The first part of the word is *tol* (short vowel)
   e. The last part of the word is *tos* (long vowel)
   f. The middle part of the word is *las* (short vowel)
   g. The first two parts of the word are *tolas*.
   h. The middle part and end of the word is *lastos*.
   i. All of the word says *tolastos*.
   j. The beginning and end of the word is *totos*.

   If your children marked *d* and *e* with an x, you are ready for the next skill. If they did not, or if they marked other questions with an x, take a new "word" and repeat all the exercises, beginning with number 2. Use this new word:

   fonesfus

   Notice that this word follows the same pattern as the first one. The beginning syllable is two letters long and the vowel has the long sound; the second and third syllables have three letters each, the vowel is in the middle, and the vowels have the short sound. Use this pattern in all the "words" you use until the children can grade your test perfectly.

10. Now use some words with different patterns:

    rustalis   mitafi   kufta

    and any other combination of syllables you want to use.

11. This exercise is to help your children to learn to see the syllables in a word quickly and well. Take one of the three-syllable words you have been working on.

Tell your children you want them to make a new word by taking the:

a. last syllable and putting it first. What does it say now?
b. middle syllable and putting it last.
c. first syllable and putting it last.
d. last syllable and putting it first; middle syllable and putting it first. (This is quite a trick. Better try it yourself first.)

12. Write a word of three syllables on the chalkboard. Put a number above each syllable:

1 2 3
tulfastol

Ask these questions:

a. What is the first syllable? Wait for the children to say it. This is the first time you have asked for a verbal response. Good. They are ready now.
b. What is the last syllable?
c. What is the middle syllable?
d. Read the first and last syllables together.
e. Read the first and second syllables together.
f. Read the first, the last, and the middle syllables in that order. (*tultolfas*)
g. Read the middle, first, and last.
h. Read the middle, first, last, first.
i. Now say just the syllables you want, such as 3, 1, 2, 3 (*toltulfastol*). Do this with several number combinations.
j. Erase the numbers, leaving only the word. Repeat exercises 1 to 9. That is, ask the same questions again.

Each day, take a new word and repeat all these exercises with it. As your children become very good at reading "words" you make up, you may ask them to make up some words for you to read. Don't urge them to do this if they seem reluctant. Instead give them some practice in making syllables. This is the way you will do it. Write these letters on the blackboard:

t l s f m

1. Ask your children to show you with their hands where the o (short) is in *tos*. "Show me with your hand which vowel says 'o.' "

2. Write the o on the blackboard with a scribble in front of it and another after it, as you did in other scribble writing. Tell your children, "This says *tos*. Let's see if we can find out what the first part is in *real* writing. Does *tos* begin like this?" (Point to the letter s.) "Does it say *tos* now? (Write the letter s where you have the scribble in front of the o.) No, that says *sos*. (Erase the s.) Does this say *tos*? (Point to another letter and repeat the procedure until the correct beginning is found.) Now that says *tos*, and that's the way it begins in real writing."

3. Say to your children, "Let's see how *tos* ends in real writing." Repeat the entire procedure with the ending sound as you did for the beginning sound.

4. Do this same thing with other syllables in which the vowel remains the same but the consonants are changed. Such syllables would be *lof, som, mot, fom,* and other similar syllables.

In these exercises with syllables, you are using an important thinking skill. You are teaching your children to use *paired comparisons*. Later in this book, you will do further work with paired comparisons to develop your children's thinking skills for reading.

Learning to Write Real Words

You may now begin to help your children write what they hear in actual words. You will use exactly the same procedure you used in teaching them to write syllables, but this time you will not list the letters to be used. Suppose you want to show them how to write *boat*. Do it this way:

> Say to them, "I want to write the word boat. Show me with your hands where the o is in boat." Write the o on the chalkboard. "Now, I want to write the first part of the word. How can I write *bo*? Now I have *bo*. How can I write the rest of the word? How can I make it boat?" Ignore the a in the word *boat* at this time. Your children cannot hear the a in boat. They are writing only the things they hear.

In helping your children to write real words, start with familiar one-syllable words that have long vowel sounds. Use such words as *road, game, kite, tube, team*.

Then use one-syllable words that have short vowel sounds, such as *run, man, sit, get, six*.

Finally, use real words of more than one syllable, but use each syllable as though it were a short word. In the word *potato,* start by having them tell you what to write for *po*.

Accept whatever the child tells you to write. If he uses an incorrect letter, he needs more practice in writing syllables. He is not expected to be perfect every time. He is learning a skill. Every time a child makes an error, it shows something *you* are doing wrong or too fast. Think what it is and go back and teach that skill some more. You cannot teach too much, but it is easy to teach too little.

Now you may begin to encourage your children to write all the things they hear in their scribble stories. Begin with only a few words from each story. As you type the words you have selected, call the child's attention to the way it begins and ends and encourage him to write the words in his story in real writing. Do not encourage him to put in the letters he does not hear. In the word *boat,* he is not expected to put in the a at this time. If he does, let it go without comment.

Gradually, your children's scribble stories will become phonetic transcriptions. This means they will write in all the sounds they hear in real words. This will take place slowly; don't rush it. The scribble story is supposed to give the child the feel of talk flowing onto paper. You can destroy this effect completely by insisting that he put in the actual letters before he is ready. Just take two or three words from each scribble story and show him how to put in the letters he hears. When he begins to do this without being told, praise him. Go on—overdo it! Praise him until he glows!

Using Context to Determine the Meaning of Words

The procedure to be used in teaching this skill can best be demonstrated by giving you an actual lesson in getting meaning from context.

Take the sentence: *The bear anskered into the forest.*

1. What do you suppose *anskered* means?

2. Make a list of all the things it could mean:

fled	walked	scrambled
lumbered	ran	skipped
went		

3. All of these words would make sense in the sentence. Which one is the correct one? Suppose this is a fat bear. *Lumbered* would make you see a fat bear. Suppose he is a *frightened* bear. Fled would make you see a frightened bear. Suppose the bear is in a hurry. *Ran* would be a good choice.

You have used two clues to get a strange word. You know *anskered* means something a bear does. The second clue is something your particular bear did. He isn't just any bear. He is the bear you are talking about.

Both of these clues involve meaning. There is a third clue: the sound of the letters in the word. This is not a meaning clue because these sounds do not have meaning except in relationship to a meaning you already have. Therefore, phonetic clues are used for precision in conveying a meaning you already have. We will not use phonetic clues in establishing the meaning of words. Since more than one word, however, can have about the same meaning, we will use phonetic clues after meaning is determined. Just keep this in mind. The sound of a word, related to the way it feels when you say it, helps you remember it.

The material you will use in teaching this skill is any sentence from which you take one word and substitute a made-up word. Take out the same kind of word each time. First take out verbs. Later take out only adjectives. Here are some examples:

Taking out verbs:

The boy went to school
The boy sofus to school.

The dog chased a cat.
The dog rultos a cat.

Taking out adjectives:

The storekeeper was a fat man.
The storekeeper was a talom man.

Jimmy is a smart boy.
Jimmy is a bamis boy.

Now let's begin.

1. Tell your children you will play a guessing game. You will guess what some words mean. The first word is *bamis.*

2. Write the word *bamis* on the chalkboard and say it again while your children look at it.

3. Now say, "Jimmy is a *bamis* boy." What do you suppose *bamis* means? What kind of boy is Jimmy?

4. Make a list of all the words your children suggest and put in a few of your own. Don't use strange words at this time. Use words your children can suggest and words you have heard them use. You are teaching a skill.

5. Now help your children select a meaning from their list. Suppose the word *fat* is on their list. You might say, "Jimmy is very big and round. What kind of boy is

Jimmy?" Accept any response your children give. Precision comes with skill and not while you are learning it. If a child offers a meaning, no matter how wrong the answer is, he is learning. He is working with meanings of his, not yours. Select another word from the list of possible meanings and repeat step 5. Do this with all the words from the list. Work with adjectives for this lesson. In the next lesson, use verbs. Then in the next lesson, go back to adjectives. When your children become good at selecting meanings for adjectives and verbs, use other parts of speech. This is not essential. They can learn this skill quite well with adjectives and verbs alone. Do not try to teach them what an adjective or a verb is. Naming is the end of an experience, not the beginning.

6. After your children have had five or six lessons with adjectives and verbs, and after they have become quite good at selecting words to fit the sentence, you can begin to use phonetic clues. Don't rush things. Your children need plenty of experience with exercises 1—5 before they start to concern themselves with phonetic clues or the way the word starts. This is the way you will teach them phonetic clues:

   The boys raced to the movies.
   The boys rafus to the movies.

   Use *rafus* exactly as you did other words in exercises 1—5. If your children do not suggest the word *race* or *raced* in the list, put in one of your words. You will use the sentence, "The boys were in a big hurry," as your clue. Ask your children to select a word from the list that begins like the made-up word. The made-up word begins *ra*.

Remember this, all words begin with a consonant and a vowel working together. If the vowel has the long sound, you will need two letters for your phonetic clue. If the vowel has the short sound, you will need two or three. Here are some examples: *Tired* could be written *tilus* but not *talus* because it begins *ti*. *Ambles* could be written *amsufa* but not *aftosu* because it begins *am*. *Getting* could be written *getlasg* but not *gatimrl* because it begins *get*.

Your children are using phonetic clues in their scribble stories because you have been helping them to put down all the sounds they hear in a few words from each story. So, in this exercise, you have only to use what they already know. They have been using syllables in their talking since they said their first word, and in their reading since they learned their first letter, because the names of the consonants are syllables.

Since your children started to talk, they have learned many new words. They learned all these new words by a combination of experimenting with how it felt to say them, hearing them said, and associating the feel and sound of these words with meaning. When they learned to say "ma-ma," they'd been saying the vowel sound ever since they were born. All they had to learn to say that word was to open and close their lips before the vowel sound. This happened because they'd been using their lips for eating both their food and their fists. But when they said, "mama," their mother came and she was pleased. The child learned to associate the word "mama" with the feel of the lip movement, the appearance of mother, and the sound of her voice when she said, "Here's mama!" These were motor, auditory, and visual perceptions working together to help the child learn to talk with meaning.

This is exactly how you are to teach them to learn new words they read and hear. They will feel them when they write them, and hear them both because you will say them and because you have taught them to associate the feel of letters with the sounds they represent. And because reading uses visual symbols or letters, they will see them just as they saw their mother when they said "mama." This is how to do it:

1. When your children hear a new word on television, in stories you read to them, or anywhere they are during the day, have them put down all the sounds they hear in the word. Remember, they will put down the sounds they hear, not the sounds you hear.

2. After a child has put down all the sounds he hears, write his word on the chalkboard exactly the way he has it on his paper. Say the word while he looks at it and have him see if he has written down all the sounds he hears.

3. Use the word in sentences and have your children tell you what it means. Write these meanings beside the word. This is getting the meanings by context as they learned to do earlier. They are using this skill. Find as many meanings as possible. The most useful thing a child can know about a word is how to pronounce it. The second most useful thing a child can know about a word is to know a number of meanings. If he can't pronounce it, he won't remember it. If he doesn't know a number of meanings, he can't use it.

4. Now go on to three or four other new words and do the same thing. After your children have about five new words, give them practice in saying them. This will help them feel the word just as writing down the sounds helped them feel it. This time, however, you will associate the feel of the word with its meaning. Say to your children, "Tell me which word means . . . ." Put in one of the words they have listed as a meaning and have your children say the new word. Do this with all five words in their list until they can say each one accurately and easily.

Perhaps you are saying, "When will my children learn to spell the new words correctly so they can read them?" No matter how many letters are in a word, a child reads only the letters that have sounds and he says only the letters that have sounds. He recognizes words he reads by the letters that have sounds. You, yourself, can read many words that you cannot spell. Spelling all the letters in a word is a visual skill, not a listening skill. To insist upon the spelling of new words at this time will actually weaken a child's ability to hear and read them. If your children had to learn to spell all the new words as they learned to talk, they'd not be talking yet. In fact, they'd probably never learn to talk. Your children are getting ready to learn to spell. They should use their new words freely and easily in their talk before any effort is begun to teach them to spell them. For the present, *forget spelling*. You will work on that in a later skill.

CHAPTER 11

Developing the Thinking Skills in Reading

The Child's Readiness in Speech

In this chapter you will work with your children's thinking skills to insure that their reading will have meaning for them. Before you get started on the thinking skills, however, here are a few reminders about maintaining the skills your children have already developed:

Continue working on the skills developed in Chapters Nine and Ten until your children can do these things easily.

Have them read aloud to you for a few minutes each day from the book you are using in your basal reading program. If they have difficulty with a word, say it for them in syllables. "That word says con ti nu," you say, while the child puts his finger under the word and looks at it. Give the vowels the sounds they have normally when you say the word. Do not explain to a child that this word is an exception to his rule. Do not explain anything. As the child gains experience in reading, he will learn most exceptions just as you did. Now give a simple definition, such as, "Continue means to go on." Stop there. When a child reads a book, he is reading to hear things. You should not spoil this. Just remember, don't ask a child to do anything about an unfamiliar word in a book. Make a note of the word and make a guess as to why it troubled him. Then review that skill in your next teaching period with him.

Continue reading to your children and continue having them write each day. These are maintenance skills and help the child to learn to use the skills you have taught him. The time will come when he will not want you to read to him. He'll want to do his own reading. And he will continue to read for the remainder of his life.

Continue having a reading period during which each child can read a book of his own. You keep on getting books to read for yourself in this period. Let the children alone. They need this time to explore books.

The Most Important Factor in Reading Comprehension

The thinking skills used in reading are no different from the thinking skills one uses in any other activity. But the ability to think grows and develops just like anything else a child learns to do. Thinking skills can be improved with a little teaching.

The most important factor in reading comprehension is the ability to see how one thing relates to another. Everything about reading relates to something else and forms a pattern. You have already seen that, in learning to read, a child related each new thing he was learning to the things he had already learned. Even the letters in a word relate to each other in a special pattern. Three thinking skills are fundamental in showing how ideas relate to each other in reading. These skills are *categories, link thinking,* and *paired comparisons*. These are the thinking skills you will teach your children in the exercises that follow.

The First Thinking Skill: Categories

1. Start with categories. Your children will use this first thinking skill to put together groups of words that stand in a special relationship of some kind. Many words used every day stand for categories. Some of these are *animals, furniture, toys, games,* and *food*. You could add hundreds more to the list. Each word calls to mind many words that relate to each other in a special way.
   Start by asking your children to name all the words they can think of that go together in a category:

   > "Name all the toys you can think of."
   > "Name all the animals you can think of."
   > "Name all the food you can think of."

   As the children name the things that go in each category, make a list of them on paper. Add a few of your own to each category. Now mix up the words in the three lists and read them back to your children. Have them put them in the category where they belong.

2. Make a picture of a cupboard with three shelves. Tell your children you will put away the groceries. Ask them to tell you where to put each thing. Now read a list of groceries to them. After each item, ask them where it would go. Write the word on the shelf they designate. Use words that classify easily, such as breads, canned goods, and things used in cooking (salt, shortening).

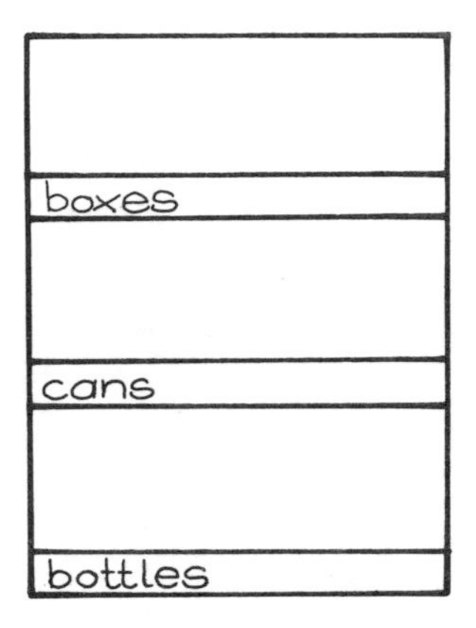

3. When you read to your children, stop now and then and use words from the story to make a category. "Jim is going fishing," you may say. "Name all the things you can think of that he will take along." Any noun or verb in the story is material for a category. Suppose a word in the story is *car*. Say to your children, "Name all the other things you can use that are ways of getting from one place to another," or "Name all the things you can think of that have wheels."

4. Begin to collect categories you can use with your children. Here's how you can make them up: Take a word and think of its opposite. Then put any other word you wish with it. Here are some to get you started:

hot-cold and animals
summer-winter and people
day-night and buildings
happy-sad and kinds of work

Now take any one of these and list them on paper like this:

hot cold animals

Put things that are hot under the first heading; things

that are cold under the second heading; names of animals under the third heading. Now number the items in all three categories so they'll be mixed up when you read them, like this:

hot	*cold*	*animals*
2 coffee	3 snow	8 dog
4 fire	1 icicles	9 pony
6 stove	5 ice	10 cat
	4 sleet	11 chicken

Notice that the words in the third category follow in order. This is so your children can identify the first two categories without having to keep a third one in mind until the pattern is established. After they have become quite good at handling two categories, you can also mix up the third list.

5. Use the categories you have made up in this way: Read the first word and ask your children to write it. Read the second word and ask them if it goes with the first word. When they say it does not, be sure to ask them why. They're likely to tell you the first word is "food" or something to drink; they'll say snow is "something that comes in winter," or "something white" or even "something cold." Tell them you will read other words that go with the first word and other things that go with the second word. You want them to write each word where it belongs. Continue reading the words and waiting for them to write each one where it belongs. They may not use the categories you have in mind. There are other ways to classify these words. Accept any classification they suggest as long as they can tell you why.
   You are teaching your children to see classification and to construct relationships; not to accept them. These are important perceptual skills.
   After your children have all the words in three lists, have them write a name for each list.

6. When your children become skillful at putting lists of words into categories, show them how to make categories of their own. Let them read their lists to you and you put them into three columns and name them.

There are many opportunities to use this skill in your everyday activities. If you plan a picnic, let your children make lists so nothing will be forgotten. They will need a list of food, a list of things to sit on, a list of games to play. A shopping list can include items under three kinds of stores: clothing stores, hardware stores, grocery stores. A grocery list can be classified under the headings: breakfast foods, luncheon foods, dinner foods. Decisions make wonderful opportunities for categories. Suppose the question is whether your children can go out to play on a rainy day. Before you decide, ask them to make a list of reasons why they should go out, and reasons why they should not.

The Second Thinking Skill: Paired Comparisons

Your children are getting pretty good at seeing categories in their reading and in their world. Now it is time to start working with another skill that will help them develop their visual skills for thinking about ideas. This skill is called paired comparisons. It's not a new skill to your chidlren. They used it, along with other thinking skills, in learning to talk. Now you will relate it directly to reading and writing. You will use it to help them see word form accurately. It will be useful to them in learning new words and it will help them become good spellers.

Take any word you'd like your children to be able to spell. Say it and have them write it in sounds as they hear it. Check by having them look at their word while you say it over slowly.

When they are satisfied that their word sounds right, put it on the chalkboard exactly as they have written it. Beside it, you write the same word correctly spelled. Now ask your children, "How are those two words *alike*?" Don't allow your children to concentrate on differences. Insist that they tell you what both words have. They both have letters. They both have sounds. They both start with the same letter. Continue in this way until you have exhausted all the ways you can think of in which both words are alike. Then ask your children, "How can we make these words exactly alike?"

At this point you will need an exercise that will help you teach your children to deal with exceptions in reading. Exceptions are those oddities in spelling that won't fit rules. No matter what and how many rules you teach your children, there are going to be instances where the rules simply won't apply. This is because language is a dynamic, human thing, and human things aren't predictable and consistent . . . especially in the way they talk. A native Georgian doesn't talk like a native of Brooklyn. In fact, no two natives of Georgia talk alike. Then too, our language is derived from many old languages, and traces of the ancestor language remain in our spelling.

Your children will deal with exceptions without any help from you. This is because of a learning behavior that is called motor-perceptual match. It means your children match up what they hear and have learned to feel in talking with what they see. It means that if they have learned to say and hear *pneumonia,* and to match the vowels and consonants they see in the printed word with their hearing and speaking, they'll see the letter p at the beginning of this, but it won't confuse them because what they say matches better with the next two letters or the first sound syllable of the word.

Now and then, something will come along in a child's reading that he may not straighten out. When that happens, he probably won't even know he isn't saying it accurately. Telling him it is wrong won't change anything. Why? Because the error is built right into his speech and can't be changed through your speech.

This is the way to deal with these errors or exceptions. Don't teach the error. Work with the skills your children have and build the skill that is missing. You won't know what skill is missing, because it is in the children's speech experiences, not yours. What you do know is what they need in order to solve their own problem. They need to match what they hear and say with what they see. You have taught your children two thinking skills that are highly visual in nature, or that use a lot of seeing. These skills are paired comparisons, or the "They both have" game, and categories, or the "Name all the things" game. When your children learn these two skills, they can combine them with their ability in sounds to learn exceptions.

Do it this way:

1. The next time your children make an error in reading that can't be handled simply by hearing the sounds of the vowels with the consonants, make a note of this error. Some examples of this type of error are *ton* when they see *tion,* saying *pone* when they see *phone* at the beginning of a word. You can think of many others. When you were taught to read, you had a long list of rules for such exceptions. You had to learn a new rule for every exception. You aren't going to give your children a rule—you'll give them a skill. It will help them deal with other exceptions without help from you. Don't work with the error at the time your children make it. Save this for another work period.

2. Let's suppose your children have made an error in the *tion* ending of a word like condition, and you know they haven't made the connection between how the ending is spelled and how it is said. You've made a note of it, and now it is another work period and you are ready to straighten out this error. To do this you'll need a list of words that contain the *tion* ending. Four to six words are fine. Using your list:

   a. Show the children how they sound.
   b. Show them how they look.
   c. Show them how they are alike.
   d. Show them what other words belong in this category.

   Your children can do all this themselves. Of course! You don't solve problems with new tools. Show your children how to use the tools they already have.

3. Dictate the words to your children and have them write them the way they sound. They'll write the endings as *shun*.

4. Write the list of such "sound" words on the chalkboard. Check each one as you go along by saying it aloud when your children look at it and letting them put in any sounds they may have left out. They're matching what they hear with what they feel when they write.

5. Now make another list of words beside the list of "sound" words. This will be a list of the same words correctly spelled. Ask your children how the two lists are alike. This is the "They both have" game your children already know. Don't explain anything. Your children have to learn this with their own speech, ears, and eyes.

6. After they have exhausted all the ways the words are alike, ask them how all the endings in the first list are alike. Ask them how all the endings in the second list are alike. Ask them how they can make the endings in the two lists exactly alike. They may suggest all the words by changed to *shun*. That's all right. Many good educators are suggesting that we change such exceptions so they're spelled the way they sound. Ask the children to tell you another way the endings in both lists can be made alike.

7. You taught your children how to put words into a category. Now put this skill to work. Ask them to take a book and find other words that end this way. Say the words aloud for them, so they can hear them say *shun* at the end. Have them look at them while you say them, so they can see how the ending looks.

Every time an exception gives your children trouble, teach it this way. They will become good spellers while they are becoming good readers because they hear the sound pattern, see the visual pattern, and correct the sound image through their own eyes. After you've taught them to do it this way, they will do it as habit every time they see a new word in reading, on a poster, on television. Spelling will become like reading: not a subject to be studied for a few minutes each day, but a way of thinking that goes on all the waking hours of your children's lives.

The Third Thinking Skill: Linked Thinking

The next thinking skill you will teach your children is called linked thinking. This is a way of putting things together so that they relate to each other in an on-going chain of ideas.

In a category, ideas cluster together. In linked thinking, they hold hands. You may have played the game you are now going to teach your children. Most people call it an association chain. However, this term is likely not to mean too much to your children, so call it the "reminds me of" game. Your children will use it for the rest of their lives in making outlines for papers they will write and talks they will make. They will use it in recalling what they have linked and in thinking out things. It serves two important thinking purposes:

1. It helps a person to remember ideas in a related pattern.

2. It helps him call up and relate ideas he knows to new ideas.

To teach your children to remember ideas in a related pattern, this is what you will do:

1. Say to your children, "Dogs remind me of barking. What do dogs remind you of?"
   Use other paired comparisons in the same way. Here are some examples:
   Breakfast reminds me of cereal. What does breakfast remind you of?
   Rain reminds me of raincoats. What does rain remind you of?
   Television reminds me of the news. What does television remind you of?
   Work on this throughout a whole day. Every time something comes up that is to be remembered, put it in this fashion: "That telephone call reminds me of your dentist appointment. What does it remind you of?" Don't worry if it reminds your children of nothing. Just keep doing it. You are setting up a thinking habit, not just getting the answer to a question.

2. On the following day, add another link to your chain of ideas. Say something like this to your children: "The telephone call reminded me of your appointment, and your dental appointment reminded me of getting out the car. What did it remind you of?" If your children add only one thing to their chain, prod gently. Say, "And

what did that remind you of?" Keep working with two-link ideas until your children are doing them easily. They may at this time start adding others without urging. If they do not, work the next day on a three-link chain of ideas.

3. Keep slowly adding links to the chain until your children go four or five links without urging from you. Take it slowly. This is an advanced thinking skill and may develop very slowly.

4. After your children are making a chain of ideas of four or five links, have them write a chain. This is the way they will do it: Think of a four-linked chain of your own. Suppose you thought, "Water reminds me of swimming, and swimming reminds me of a bathing suit, and a bathing suit reminds me of sunshine." Fine. Sit beside your children and write the key words in a list on a sheet of paper.

   water
   swimming
   bathing suit
   sunshine

   Now point to water and say, "Water reminds me of swimming." Point to swimming and say, "Swimming reminds me of bathing suits." Keep on this way, pointing to each key word, until you have read your chain.

5. Now it is your children's turn to do exactly the same thing with a chain of their own. If they have difficulty with this, go back to the two-word chain, only this time write it on paper as you did with the four-word chain. Have your children do the same thing.

6. When they can write a two-linked chain quite easily, add another link as you did when you were saying the words aloud. Keep on adding links until your children can add five or six links to their thinking.

7. Keep alert to opportunities to use linked thinking in situations in your daily life. We have already talked about the various events of the day that give you a chance to practice linked thinking.

8. Now begin to use linked thinking with stories you read aloud to your children. This ability is very useful in recalling material you have read. After you have read a story to your children, take an important word from the first part of the story and use it to start a chain of ideas. Suppose you have just finished *Jack and the Beanstalk*. One of the most important events in the first part of the story had to do with Jack's selling the cow for a handful of beans. So start your chain with "Cows remind me of . . ." and let your children take it from there. If they have any difficulty, use a few supporting questions, such as: "What happened to the cow in the story?" Jack sold the cow for some beans. Fine. "Cows remind me of sold, and sold reminds me of beans, and beans reminds me of . . ." At this point your chain is well under way.

   If your children need further help to recall the events of the story in an idea chain, do this: Take one paragraph from the story and read the first sentence. Ask your children to pick one word from the sentence and write it down. They can pick any word they want to pick. Don't prod them to select the word you think they should pick. The ability to see the pattern of ideas in a selection is complex and difficult and requires much experience in dealing with ideas. Your children are just learning this skill, but they must learn it themselves. You can't learn it for them. Take each sentence in the paragraph. Read it aloud. Have your children pick one word and write it down. Then have them read their idea chain aloud. It may not be a very good idea chain, but it is a beginning. It is giving your children the feel of selecting words from the story.

The second important thinking purpose of idea chains is to help your children call up and relate ideas they know to new ideas. Now you will give your children one word and have them make an idea chain from it. After they have made their idea chain, ask them to write a story using it. You can also have your children make their own idea chain from the start by asking them to name one word that is a —. Put in any word you wish. You could use color, animal, food, game, or piece of clothing. You could use any noun in the English language. When your children have named the word, ask them to write it down. Suppose you say, "Name one word that is a piece of clothing," and your children say "coat." After they have written coat on their paper, say to them, "What does coat remind you of? Write that. What does used (the second word they have written) remind you of? Write that." Keep this up for five or six words. Then ask your children to put their paper aside and do these things:

1. Name all the words in the list in order.
2. Name the third word in the list.
3. Name the first and last word in the list.
4. Name the first, third, and last word in the list.
5. Name all the words backwards.

After they have done all these things, have them write a story using all the words in the list.

When your children wrote their first scribble stories, they planned them in advance by drawing a picture to show what the stories were going to be about. This was the first outline.

Now they are going to use idea chains as a basis for a more advanced outline.

1. First have them make an idea chain of five or six words. Have them write this chain on paper. Suppose the idea chain is about animals and your children have written: dogs, cats, rabbits, cows, horses, pigs.
2. Write the first word from their idea chain on the chalkboard. Ask them to tell you everything they know about dogs. List their ideas under the word *dogs*. Dogs make good pets. Dogs bark. There are many kinds of dogs.
3. Do the same thing with each word in the idea chain. Number the words in the idea chain like this:

a. dogs
bark
make good pets
there are many kinds

b. cats
scratch
are soft
catch mice

4. After all the words in the idea chain have been developed in this way, say to your children, "Tell me about your dogs." Select any word from the idea chain for this telling activity. After your children have finished telling you about the word, say to them, "Now look at your outline and see if you have forgotten anything."

Expanding Word Meanings Through Writing and Listening

At this point, we will work on a method of helping your children build a rich and varied vocabulary. They will not need to learn a new skill for this, but they will use every skill they have learned. Using the skills in this way will not only help them learn new words, but it will also strengthen all skills that make them good readers.

A good vocabulary helps your children get meaning from what they read. It helps them express their ideas more easily. It helps them think about ideas. Not the least in importance, it helps them communicate so that others appreciate and enjoy them. This then means your children will gain greater pleasure from sharing ideas. Sharing ideas will give them constant practice in the abilities needed to share ideas. All of this adds up to a finer life for your children.

A good vocabulary is more than knowing many words. The effective person is the one who knows exactly the right word to use in a situation. You will help your children learn about many words and much about each word as they learn it. The more meanings a child has for a word, the more valuable it will be to him.

The only difficult thing about this exercise is choosing the words your children need to learn. You can't just choose words you yourself need to learn because your words often represent experiences your children have not had and are not ready to have. A child should learn the meanings of words that he needs in order to tell you about something, the words he needs in order to understand what he reads, and the words he needs in order to write what he wants to write.

There are three sources of words you will use. First, listen carefully when your children try to tell you something. When they struggle to express an idea, think of a word that would help. List that word for the next word-study lesson. Often a teacher will say to a child, "Oh, you mean . . ." That's the word you will make a note of for a lesson. Sometimes the child says, "No, not that. I mean . . ." He is telling you he doesn't have the exact words he needs to express an idea. Make a note of the word that would help him.

Second, writing is talking on paper. You will notice exactly these same things in stories your children write. When they say to you, "How would you say . . ." or "How would you write . . .", they are struggling for words. Make a note of words that would help them. Sometimes your children will stop in the middle of reading a story they have written and add ideas aloud. They are expressing a need for certain words that did not come easily to them when they were writing. What words would help here?

Third, listen to your children read aloud for a few minutes each day. Many words we use do not fit any phonetic pattern because no two people ever talk in exactly the same way. However, all say those words in pretty much the same way because we match what we say with what we see in print. A very common example is the word *said*. If we followed the rules, we would use a long sound for the vowel a and the i would be silent. What we actually say is *sed*. That's because the word is in our speaking vocabulary and just a few clues in the way it looks in print make us know what it really is. However, if the word isn't in a child's speaking vocabulary, he won't make the adjustment of sight to sound. He will read *pneumonia* with the first syllable *pu*, or *canoe* will be *cano*. These are not mistakes. They are signals that the words are not in a child's *meaning vocabulary*. When he knows the meaning of a word, he will use it, hear other people use it, and match what is said to what he sees. He will do this because you have trained his body to feel words, his ears to hear sounds, and his eyes to see patterns. So when your children make errors in pronouncing words in reading, list those as words they need to know the meaning of.

Any time your children ask, "What does that word mean?", tell them and then add that word to your list.

Now you are ready to help your children add these new words to their reading vocabulary. This is how you will do it:

1. Select a few words from your list—not more than five, not less than three. Tell your children you will read a

list of words and you want them to write them. Read the words aloud and have your children write all the things they think they hear in the word.

2. Now match the sound word with the sight word as you did in teaching them to spell. After you have done this, give your children practice in pronouncing the words. What does the third word say? What does the first word say?

3. Use the word in sentences to show several meanings and have your children guess what the word means in each sentence. Write these new meanings by the word.

4. Finally, use the meaning and ask the children to give the word. "What word from your list means *happy*?"

Remember this: If a word is to be a true part of a child's working vocabulary, he must hear it, and say it, before he sees it.

There are many sources of new words for your children's vocabularies. However, three sources are most useful for their reading vocabulary in their first ten years.

First, the names of things, or nouns. When your children learn a name for something, that name is like a category. It stands for many experiences. Every time they use the name, all the other experiences come to mind and help them understand. The word *dog,* for example, stands for all the dogs they have owned, their playmates' dogs, dogs they have seen on television and in books, how they feel about dogs, and all the things they know about dogs from hearing them, feeling them, seeing them.

When your children first started learning to talk, they learned names for things, or nouns, such as *mama, daddy, ball, baby*. These names acted as organizers or subjects around which they could learn and remember other ideas. All of your children's experiences are built around a special vocabulary of names. When they take a vacation they will learn such names as *motel, road map, luggage,* and many other such words. These are very important to them. You can help by teaching the proper names for experiences your children have had. A trip to the dentist, a walk in the park, a vacation trip, a new pet, a birthday—all of these experiences can be remembered and used again and again if your children learn the vocabulary of the experience or the names of the things they experience.

Second, words that do things, or verbs. Another class of words that is of great value to your children in developing their reading vocabulary is *verbs*. Verbs get things going in a sentence, so help your children get their thinking moving by enriching their stock of action words.

When your children first learned to talk, they used many verbs very early. Along with mama and daddy, they started using such words as go, walk, play, and words that are a combination of a name and an action, such as drink. Having many verbs at one's command lends color and power to one's thinking.

Third, how things look, or adjectives. The third class of most useful words for the children's vocabulary is words that make them see what they are reading about, or *adjectives*. Much of a child's pleasure in reading comes from his ability to see what is going on in a story and thus to identify and feel with the characters. A story without this quality is like a television program without a picture. One can understand the story but one has difficulty in feeling it.

Again, adjectives came rather early into a child's speech. Even before he could say them he learned the feel, and therefore the meaning, of many adjectives. Words such as: *good* boy, *pretty* ball, and *nice* dinner were used early to identify how he was to feel about his world. Notice that these words are used first in conjunction with name words. Another way of saying it is that adjectives help a child see his reading and care about it.

These three classes of words then, adjectives, nouns, and verbs, help your children organize their thinking, see the ideas in a story, and get right up in front where the action is. They are the raw material of thinking and, therefore, the best source of new words for your children's vocabulary. Along with many other words your children will learn, see that they get liberal doses of nouns, adjectives, and verbs.

Here is a good way to help your children put their nouns, verbs, and adjectives to work in their reading. Use their ability to make categories in building a storehouse of words. Work together with your children to make lists of words that help one see, another of words that show what one is doing, another list that is names of things. For these lists use words your children already know. Keep the list handy. As they learn new words, add them to the list. When one list gets much longer than another, plan with your children to listen for words that can be put on the shorter list. You will be building their skill in categorizing information.

After your children have three fairly long lists of words, start using these lists in their writing. Take one word from the list of things, or nouns, about which to write a story. List other things that will go into the story. Now, what does each word look like? You will need words from the see list, or adjectives. What will each thing do in the story? You will need words from the do list, or verbs. Your children suggest words that are not on the lists? Wonderful! Add them to the lists.

Now let them write their story in any way they please. Don't require them to stick to the original list of words. Often these lists serve only to stimulate your children's thinking.

Teaching the Child How to Ask Questions

We are now ready to consider a final thinking skill that is important to your children's ability to comprehend what they read. Learning to ask questions is just as important as being able to answer them. When you check your children's ability to understand what they have read, you ask them questions and listen to their answers. The answers are what the child has after he has read. The questions that he asked himself as he read determine the answers he got from his reading. Asking the right question takes a person half way to the answer.

The ability to ask questions is one that develops slowly. Your children started asking questions early in their lives. In fact, most parents say their children drive them crazy with their questions. Then why teach them to ask them? Questions must bear a direct relationship to what is given in the material and what is needed by the reader. The questions your children can ask are determined in large part by their understanding of how sentences are put together. When your children try to understand written material, they must deal with the meanings of words and the order in which they are used. They must also understand something of the intentions of the writer. If one were to read this sentence:

I hate you

he would interpret it according to the question in his own mind and give weight to the words in the sentence accordingly. Suppose you ask yourself: Who hates me? The word "I" becomes the most important word in the sentence. Watch the importance of the words in this sentence shift as different questions are asked:

Who hates me?
I hate you.
How do you feel about me?
I *hate* you.
Whom do you hate?
I hate *you*.

The same words are used in each answer but the meaning changes with the question that was asked.

Your children must learn to ask the right questions if they are to get correct answers. They must learn to ask questions of themselves before they read and as they read. They must learn to ask questions that will direct them to the information in reading materials. They won't learn to ask questions by answering questions you ask. They must learn to ask their own and check their answers against those given in the material.

There are two important things you can do as you read to your children. The next time you read a story, do this after you have finished reading: Say to them, "I want to know if . . . (put in anything from the story that will fit). What question will I ask?" Keep doing this for several questions. When your children are giving the answers easily, stop before you tell what you want to know and see if your children will supply the rest of the statement, this way: "I want to know if . . . (wait for them to finish it)." If they do not do this, supply the rest of the statement and let them ask the question. Keep this up until your children are supplying both the subject of the question and the answer, this way: "I want to know if . . . (your children supply the rest of the sentence). What question will I ask? (your children supply the question)." Here is the second thing you can do while you are reading to your children to help them learn to ask the right questions: Before you start reading a story, say, "The story I am going to read is about . . . (you give the subject of the story). What do you suppose the book will talk about?"

If your children use statements in response to this question, help them change them into questions. Suppose they say, "It will be about how many fish George caught." Write on the chalkboard or on a sheet of paper, "1. How many fish did George catch?" Continue in this fashion until you have three or four questions. Then tell your children you will read the story and they are to put a check mark by each question the story answers. When you finish reading the story, have your children answer their questions that the story did not answer. Have them ask *you* the questions that the story did.

Here are two exercises you can use to help your children see the patterns of sentences. First, a simple example such as:

George was going fishing.

Write this sentence on the chalkboard and put a number above each word in the sentence like this:

1 2 3 4
George was going fishing.

Now ask your children to read the sentence different ways.

Give them these numbers and have them read the words under the numbers: 2, 1, 3, 4. "Was George going fishing?" Then you say after the children have read the question, "George was going fishing." Use many simple statements in this way.

The second exercise is a variation of this game. Give your children a new word and a number pattern and ask them to make questions.

Give them *who* and the pattern 2, 3, 4, to make the question, "Who was going fishing?"

Give them *where* and the pattern 2, 1, 3, to make the question, "Where was George going?"

Other words and other patterns can be used in this way. As your children gain skill in doing these things, you can help them to construct more complex questions by using more words. For example, you could give them these new words—*what* and *to do*—and the number pattern 2, 1, 3, to make the question, "What was George going to do?"

Another exercise that will help your children learn to ask questions is the "who-what" game. Again, take simple statements and ask them to ask you a question beginning with *who* and another question beginning with *what*. This exercise will help your children to focus their attention upon two important parts of the sentence (subject and predicate).

Encourage your children to use their ability to ask questions to find out about a subject. The next time they ask you a question, say, "That's an important question. The answer is —." Give them a simple, direct answer to part of their question and then say, "Was that all you wanted to know?"

If you've not completely answered the question, they'll keep asking questions. That's exactly what you want them to do!

CHAPTER 12

The Teacher's Support

As the children move into actual experience with books, the attitude and support of the teacher is highly significant. Children enjoy exploring verbal materials as they enjoyed learning to talk. Of necessity, their first efforts are clumsy and often almost amusingly inaccurate. Adults gathered together inevitably spend considerable time relating amusing episodes about the initial speech of children. However, it is observed that this same attitude isn't taken toward their children's first efforts to show independence in word perception. Too often, they do not recognize the child's right to make these inevitable initial errors in applying his developing skills to new words in print.

Much should be done to maintain the child's initial zest and potential for new words. Remember that the important factor, in his eagerness to display his skill in "getting the word all by myself," is not that he pronounced the word correctly but that he tried to apply his learning to verbal exploration and that the effort resulted in satisfaction. The teacher must recognize and support this by objective praise of the effort and not by evaluation of the success.

She must remember that children do not develop skills through being "told how." They learn by actual doing. In the reading act, the child who is learning his word perception skills has this fundamental need. He needs to have an opportunity to apply his skills to determine the pronunciation of new words. This means that all new words should not be presented orally and drilled into the child before he reads a story. It means that the teacher should have the patience to "wait him out" during his observation of a word, and restrain the impulse to jump in and offer him the word before he has had the joy of finding it for himself. To offer the word to the child is to deprive him of the essential practice of applying and refining his skills. In addition, it deprives the teacher of a rare possibility for diagnostic analysis, which may show need for further practice in essential skills.

CHAPTER 13

Helping Parents to Enjoy Having a Reader in the Family

By the time you reach this chapter, most of your children will know all the perceptual skills necessary to be a good reader. They will know how to hear words, to explore them, and to relate them to each other in the thinking patterns of their language. A child needs one more thing. He needs many years of opportunity to gain experience with using these skills. How do you help him with this? Tell his parents these things:

Relax and Enjoy Him. You have already discovered that companionship is an important factor in helping your child learn to enjoy books. You and he have spent many pleasant hours getting books from the library, reading them together, and reading to each other. Soon now, your child is going to begin to want to do more reading for himself and spend less time listening to you read to him. Perhaps you will miss this.

As the child begins to read more for himself, spend more time discussing ideas with him. One of the greatest pleasures of reading is to share what you have read with others. Let him tell you about his books, and you tell him about yours. Ask questions and answer his. Let him use reading more in his daily life. The next time you go out to eat, give him the menu instead of reading it to him. Let him read it for himself and make his own choices. If he doesn't notice the prices, call his attention to them. They are part of the information you use in making a decision. Your child needs to learn to use all available information in making a decision.

When you listen to the morning news, encourage your child to listen with you. This is a part of his background for reading. Keeping up with the world around us will help your child enjoy books more. After you have listened to the news, get the paper and compare the newscast with the report in the paper.

Your child will be listening to the news the rest of his life, and he will be reading the paper. Help him learn to enjoy these media for acquiring information.

Gradually your child will begin to develop specific interests in topics of his own selection. One of the first interests most young children show is in animals. This interest may range all the way from Peter Rabbit to prehistoric animals. Fine! Become a specialist in animals right along with your child. Show him that books will answer his questions. Don't read the books and don't answer his questions for him. Get him the books and let him find his own answers. If he can ask the question, he is ready to find the answer.

Show your child that different books present different ideas on a subject. Call his attention to the way two books vary in what is said about a subject that is of interest to your child. Discuss these things freely. But remember—discuss doesn't mean to tell him! It means you have your say and you listen politely to his say. Don't straighten him out! He will do that for himself as he reads and shares ideas with you. Children have natural good taste in books. It needs only liberal exposure to a variety of reading material and the ability to read well, plus an opportunity to share ideas, to bring out your child's good taste in books.

Keep up your own interest in reading. To really enjoy them, a child needs to learn to live with books. Reading must become a tool for living in your home, one you use every day to get information, to solve problems, and just to enjoy. Read those books you've always intended to read. Your child will imitate you. Don't let reading be something you do during a "reading period." Let it be as much a part of you as your talking. That's what books are. They are experts who will consult with you. They are good friends who will argue with you. They are artists who will entertain you. They are companions who will share with you. It's not too late for you to find this out. Your child is learning this now. Go along with him into the wonderful world of books.

VOOM

Appendix

Test for the Perceptual Skills in Reading

This is a test of the eleven developmental skills for the mechanics of reading. It should be given as a group test to make an individual analysis and plan a program for each child. Each child should be placed in a group working on the skill he needs. Thus, each child is placed in a group for a specific measurable reason. When the skill is mastered by the individual, he should be moved to another group working on a skill he needs.

All tests are auditory except Tests X and XI. The child does not see the stimulus item.

TEST I

This is a test for visual recognition of all the letters of the alphabet. Use all lower-case letters and include all of the 26 letters.

Teacher's Key	Sample Test					
c	1.	a	h	c	f	d
n	2.	s	p	l	n	o

Directions: "Put your finger under number 1. Across, in that row, you will see 5 letters. Circle the letter I say."

Correcting: In case of error, *circle the correct answer on child's test.* Teach the circled letters.

TEST II

This is a test for where a child hears the vowel name (long vowel) in a word or syllable; either at beginning (B), middle (M), or at the end (E) of the syllable. Nonsense syllables are used to avoid giving visual clues.

Teacher's Key	Sample Test (Use 12 Items)	B	M	E
nake	1.	—	—	—
afe	2.	—	—	—
na	3.	—	—	—
stay	4.	—	—	—

Directions: "We're going to play a game, X marks the spot. Put an X on the line going across, which shows where you hear the "a" in nake."

Correcting: If there is a cluster of three errors or more, this skill needs to be retaught.

TEST III

This is a test for the visual identification of the long vowel names.

Teacher's Key		Sample Test (Use 12 Items)				
fay	1.	a	e	i	o	u
mean	2.	a	e	i	o	u
tie	3.	a	e	i	o	u

Directions: "Circle the letter in line 1 that says its name in fay."
Correcting: Circle the *correct* answer in the row if the child has made an error.

TEST IV

This is to test how many things you hear in a word containing open syllables.

Teacher's Key		Sample Test (Use 12 Items)					
flay	A.	1	2	3	4	5	6
you	B.	1	2	3	4	5	6
splaink	C.	1	2	3	4	5	6

Directions: "Circle the number that tells how many things you hear in flay."

TEST V

This is a test for open syllables.

Teacher's Key		Sample Test (Use 12 Items)					
bicycle	1.	ba	be	bi	bo	bu	none
* biscuit	2.	ba	be	bi	bo	bu	none
bugle	3.	ba	be	bi	bo	bu	none

Directions: "Circle the first syllable you hear in bicycle." Use nonsense words with older children. * The first syllable in biscuit is bis.

TEST VI

This is a test for the place of vowel *sounds* (short vowels).

		Sample Test (Use 12 Items)		
Teacher's Key		B	M	E
af	1.	—	—	—
glap	2.	—	—	—

Directions: "Put an X on the line going across, which shows where you hear the a (short) in af."

TEST VII

This is a test for vowel sounds (short vowels).

Teacher's Key	Sample Test (Use 12 Items)					
af	1.	a	e	i	o	u
grep	2.	a	e	i	o	u
lup	3.	a	e	i	o	u

Directions: "What vowel says its sound in af? Circle that vowel."
Correcting: Circle the *correct* answer in case of error.

TEST VIII

This is a test for auditory recognition of the number of things heard in a word containing closed syllables.

Teacher's Key	Sample Test (Use 12 Items)						
esk	A.	1	2	3	4	5	6
ef	B.	1	2	3	4	5	6
splenk	C.	1	2	3	4	5	6

Directions: "Circle the number of things you hear in esk."

TEST IX

This is a test for auditory recognition of closed syllables.

Teacher's Key	Sample Test (Use 12 Items)						
baffle	1.	baf	bef	bif	bof	buf	none
listen	2.	las	les	lis	los	lus	none
after	3.	af	ef	if	of	uf	none
rival	4.	rav	rev	riv	rov	ruv	none

Directions: "Circle the syllable you hear at the beginning of *baffle*."
Nonsense words may also be used to avoid dependence on visual clues.

TEST X

This is a test for determining the number and kind of syllables in a word.

---

1. baffilost ( )
2. fatelasif ( )
3. regdab ( )
4. tekosin ( )
5. renneto ( )
6. emmerk ( )
7. dreksatef ( )
8. reffidener ( )
9. astilfa ( )
10. etsatcama ( )

Directions: "There are 10 words here that you've never seen before. Indicate in the bracket the number of syllables each word has. Then go back and mark long and short vowels in all the syllables."

TEST XI

Context Clues

---

1. The boys *astilfa* his books. *Astilfa* means ______________.
2. The bear *skedelfered* into the forest. *Skedelfered means* ______________.
3. We went to the *pelsak* and saw the show. *Pelsak* means ______________.
4. The girl *taseto* the tablecoth. *Taseto* means ______________.
5. Mother *dapfel* the candy. *Dapfel* means ______________.
6. The baby *femop* the ice cream cone. *Femop* means ______________.
7. The janitor will *gedrab*. *Gedrab* means ______________.
8. Jack was *tirba* as he went into school. *Tirba* means ______________.
9. Peter can go down the *nogaw* in his wagon. *Nogaw* means ______________.
10. Susan is *redun* the umbrella. *Redun means* ______________

Directions: "Here are some sentences containing strange new words. Tell what each underlined word means."

Correcting: Any answer that makes sense is acceptable.

BIBLIOGRAPHY

1. DUGGINS, LYDIA A. "A Sequential Program For the Development of Skills in Spatial Relationships and Closure as a Basis for Reading Comprehension". *The Special Education Clinic*. Southeastern Louisiana College. Research Bulletin Number 3. Hammond, Louisiana. 1958.

2. DUGGINS, LYDIA A. "Auditory Perception in the Beginning Reading Program". *The Special Education Clinic*. Southeastern Louisiana College. Research Bulletin Number 1. Hammond, Louisiana. 1955.

3. DUGGINS, LYDIA A. "Theory and Techniques of Auditory Perception as an Approach to Reading". *The Reading Teachers' Reader* edited by Oscar S. Causey. The Ronald Press Company, New York. 1958.

4. DUGGINS, LYDIA A. "Relating Reading Instruction to Children's Developmental Growth Patterns". *Vistas in Reading*, Vol. II, Part 1. Proceedings of the Eleventh Annual Convention. International Reading Association. 1967.

5. RUSSELL, DAVID H. and FEA, HENRY R. "Research on Teaching Reading", *Handbook of Research on Teaching*. American Educational Research Association. A Department of the National Education Association. Rand McNally & Company, Chicago. 1963.